Python Programming: A Logic, Problem-Solving, and Puzzle-Based Approach

Published by:

Binary Horizon Academic

United States

Companion Resources & Ordering Information:

For lecture slides, curriculum resources, textbook adoptions, or examination copies, please visit www.aymanalzaid.com or contact the author directly via the website's support channels.

FIRST EDITION

First Printing: 2026

ISBN-13: 979-8-951087-00-3 (Paperback)

ISBN-13: 979-8-951087-01-0 (eBook)

Publisher's Note:

Python and its logos are trademarks of the Python Software Foundation. All source code examples, logic puzzles, and auditing exercises in this textbook are provided solely for educational purposes, "as is," without warranty of any kind.

Suggested Citation:

Alzaid, A. (2026). *Python Programming: A Logic, Problem-Solving, and Puzzle-Based Approach*. Binary Horizon Academic.

Foreword

Computer science education is changing. The field no longer rewards students who can recite syntax from memory. It rewards students who can read unfamiliar code, spot the flaw in a logical argument, and reconstruct a broken function from first principles. These are not the skills a passive textbook produces.

This textbook does not ask you to memorize. It asks you to think. Every chapter is built on one conviction: the fastest path to genuine programming fluency is active, analytical engagement with code that challenges you, breaks your assumptions, and forces you to reason carefully about what the interpreter is actually doing.

Programming is the discipline of translating abstract human intent into precise, executable instructions. The gap between a beginner and a working engineer is not vocabulary. It is the habit of rigorous logical thinking. This book is built to close it.

Preface

The Mindset: Software Engineering

Most beginners judge their code by one standard: did it run without crashing? If yes, the script feels finished. Software engineering rejects that standard entirely. A program that runs is not automatically a program worth keeping.

Software engineering is the professional practice of building code that is functional, readable, and maintainable over the long life of a project. Think of code the way a chef thinks of a written recipe. The recipe must be accurate enough for any other trained cook to walk into the kitchen, read the instructions without confusion, and reproduce the exact same dish. Clarity is not optional. It is the core deliverable.

The technique that makes this possible is **problem decomposition**. Take a large, intimidating problem. Break it into the smallest logical pieces you can identify. Solve each piece independently. Writing code is the act of recording those solutions in a language the machine can execute. Break before build. That is the engineering mindset this book builds.

A Note from the Author: Pedagogical Philosophy

This book is built on **Active Learning**. Reading a perfectly functional program teaches you almost nothing useful. You can follow every line, nod along, and still be completely stuck the moment you face a blank file. That false confidence is the specific failure this text is designed to prevent.

Every theory section in this book is immediately followed by three distinct challenge types. You will investigate code that is intentionally broken. You will predict the output of scripts designed to test the edges of your assumptions. You will diagnose and rewrite messy scripts against professional engineering standards. Each task requires you to reason actively rather than read passively.

In my own university classrooms, these become genuinely competitive exercises. Students run the code to check whether they were right. They debate execution pathways with each other between classes. They treat the debugging tasks as games to win rather than chores to complete. The engagement level shifts completely once the material demands active participation. This book brings that same structure to independent study.

I apply these code quality and auditing activities across all of my programming language courses, whether teaching Python, C++, Java, or web technologies. Syntax varies between languages, but the demand for clean, readable, and maintainable code does not. Students who learn to spot style violations and structural problems early build habits that follow them into every language they pick up afterward. They do not just write code that runs. They write code that another engineer can read, understand, and modify without frustration.

This approach trains habits that carry across every language. Code quality and adherence to language standards are not optional in professional work, and they should not be optional in education either. This book formalizes that structure for both classroom use and independent study.

AI Resilience and Authentic Assessment

The rapid rise of Generative Artificial Intelligence has reshaped what it means to assess programming ability in higher education. When working code can be produced from a prompt in seconds, a student's ability to write boilerplate from memory is no longer the relevant measure. The relevant measure is what they can do with code they did not write: read it critically, identify what is wrong with it, explain why it fails, and fix it to professional standards.

This textbook is built as a deliberate response to that shift. Every active learning challenge in these pages requires something that language models cannot do on a student's behalf: trace a variable through a live execution environment, identify which of several nearly identical scripts contains the logical defect, or defend a refactoring decision against a specific style standard. These tasks demand authentic analytical reasoning. They cannot be completed by pasting a question into a chat window.

For educators, this creates a practical framework for maintaining academic integrity without monitoring software or proctoring tools. The exercises are not resistant to AI by restriction or lockdown. They are resistant because they require the kind of reasoning that only comes from working through the problem yourself. This book provides a curriculum built and refined through classroom practice, designed to keep assessment meaningful in an environment where code generation is free and instant.

A Note to the Developer

This workbook has no answer key.

In professional software engineering, there is no back of the book to consult when verifying a production script. The terminal is the authority. The absence of pre-written solutions is not oversight, and it is not a problem. It is the point.

To check your work on each pillar, run the code:

- **For Puzzles and Logic Exercises:** Do not guess. Write your prediction down first, tracing variable states line by line on paper. Once you have a definite answer, open your editor, type the code into a .py file, and run it. The output tells you whether your prediction was right.
- **For Code Audits:** When you refactor a poorly written or broken script, the Python interpreter is your check. If your corrected code throws a SyntaxError or IndentationError, read the traceback, find the line causing the error, and fix it yourself.

The cognitive struggle of debugging your own mental model when it disagrees with the computer console is where programming competency is built. Every missing answer is a challenge to prove your solution correct on the only platform that counts.

About the Author

Ayman Alzaid is a Professor of Computer Science who holds a Ph.D. with an interdisciplinary focus spanning Computer Science, Curriculum and Instruction, and Learning Design and Technology, alongside an M.S. in Computer Science and a B.S. with a dual major in Computer Information Science and Multimedia.

His teaching spans Python, C++, Java, C#, HTML, CSS, JavaScript, data structures and algorithms, object-oriented programming, game design, artificial intelligence, and computer animation.

His research focuses on data science, artificial intelligence, machine learning, human-computer interaction, and CS curriculum design. He is a faculty partner of the Computing Alliance of Hispanic-Serving Institutions (CAHSI) and a contributor to the Math Snacks project.

The puzzle-based, audit-driven curriculum this textbook formalizes has been developed and refined through classroom practice.

How to Use This Book

Each chapter follows the same four-part structure. **Theoretical Foundation** opens with the concept, explains how it works at the interpreter level, and shows where it connects to what you already know. **Formal Syntax** presents the exact notation Python requires. **Implementation and Code Examples** gives five programs of increasing complexity with expected output. The Active Learning Framework closes with three challenge pillars that require you to do the thinking yourself.

You need two things before you begin: a working Python installation (3.10 or later) and a code editor. **VS Code with the Python extension** is what I recommend. IDLE, which ships with every Python installation, works for every exercise if you prefer a lighter tool. Either way, every prediction you make in the Pillar 2 puzzles and every audit you complete in Pillar 3 should be verified by running the actual code. The terminal is the authority.

This workbook contains no answer keys. **That is not an oversight**. The process of predicting output, running the code, and reconciling the difference between what you expected and what happened is the learning. An answer key would short-circuit the most valuable part of each exercise. When your prediction is wrong, do not look for the answer elsewhere. Trace the code again, run it again, and find out exactly where your mental model diverged from the interpreter.

The PySurgeon Companion Tool

If you do not have a Python environment set up yet, or you are working on a machine where you cannot install software, there is a third option. PySurgeon is a free, online Python compiler built specifically as a companion tool for this course. It runs in any browser, requires no installation and no account, and executes real CPython code through a WebAssembly port of the interpreter. You can reach it at www.aymanalzaid.com/pysurgeon.

PySurgeon is not a replacement for a proper development environment. VS Code is still what I recommend for serious work. But for the trace exercises, code audits, and puzzles in this book, it does exactly what you need: you paste code, press Run, and the output tells you whether your prediction was right. It also includes a compiler report panel that shows you how Python parsed your program, which is useful when the error is not where you expected it to be.

The name is intentional. PySurgeon is built for precise, methodical diagnosis of code, which is exactly the discipline this book trains.

The Active Learning Framework

Every chapter pairs its theory section with three structured challenge pillars. Each pillar trains a different cognitive skill and builds on the one before it.

Pillar	Activity Type	What You Do	Cognitive Skill Targeted
P1 Logic	Logic Exercises	Trace variables and step through interpreter execution one line at a time.	Builds an accurate mental model of Python memory allocation and mutation.
P2 Puzzle	Mysterious Output	Predict the output of tricky edge-case scripts before executing them.	Exposes hidden edge cases and sharpens precision code-tracing.
P3 Audit	Code Audits	Diagnose and refactor poorly written scripts to PEP 8 standards.	Trains professional discipline in clean code architecture and style.

Textbook Structure

This book moves through five progressive sections. Each section builds directly on the concepts established before it. A student who works through the chapters in order will move from writing a first print statement to constructing object-oriented programs with proper exception handling.

Section	Chapters	Core Topics
Theoretical Foundation	1 – 3	Introduction to Programming and Python, Variables and Data Types, Input/Output and Arithmetic Operations
Decision Structures	4 – 6	Boolean Logic and Comparison Operators, Python Conditionals, The match-case Statement
Functions and Modularity	7 – 8	User-Defined Functions, Built-in Functions and PEP 8 Standards
Iteration and Sequences	9 – 12	Loops and Iteration, Python Lists, Strings as Sequences, Dictionaries and Tuples
Advanced Frameworks	13 – 14	Exception Handling, Object-Oriented Programming

Table of Contents

Foreword ... ii
Preface ... iii
The Mindset: Software Engineering ... iii
A Note from the Author: Pedagogical Philosophy ... iii
AI Resilience and Authentic Assessment ... iv
A Note to the Developer ... iv
About the Author ... iv
How to Use This Book ... v
The PySurgeon Companion Tool ... v
The Active Learning Framework ... vi
Textbook Structure ... vi
Introduction to Programming and Python ... 2
Theoretical Foundation ... 2
Formal Syntax and Declaration ... 4
Implementation and Code Examples ... 6
Code Quality and Professional Standards ... 9
The Active Learning Framework ... 10
Coding Challenge: Final Programming Task ... 15
Chapter Summary ... 16
Fundamentals, Variables, and Data Types ... 17
Theoretical Foundation ... 17
Formal Syntax and Declaration ... 20
Implementation and Code Examples ... 21
The Active Learning Framework ... 24
Coding Challenge: Employee Profile Builder ... 30
Chapter Summary ... 31
Input, Output, and Arithmetic Operations ... 32
Theoretical Foundation ... 32
Formal Syntax and Declaration ... 34
Implementation and Code Examples ... 35
The Active Learning Framework ... 39
Coding Challenge: Personal Finance Calculator ... 44
Chapter Summary ... 44
Boolean Logic and Comparison Operators ... 45
Theoretical Foundation ... 45
Formal Syntax and Declaration ... 49

Implementation and Code Examples 49
The Active Learning Framework 53
Coding Challenge: Event Access Validator 58
Chapter Summary 58
Python Conditionals 59
Theoretical Foundation 59
Formal Syntax and Declaration 61
Implementation and Code Examples 63
The Active Learning Framework 67
Coding Challenge: Ticket Price Calculator 73
Chapter Summary 74
The Python match-case Statement 75
Theoretical Foundation 75
Formal Syntax and Declaration 78
Implementation and Code Examples 79
The Active Learning Framework 83
Coding Challenge: Currency Exchange Desk 88
Chapter Summary 89
Functions in Python 90
Theoretical Foundation 90
Formal Syntax and Declaration 93
Implementation and Code Examples 94
The Active Learning Framework 98
Coding Challenge: Student Grade Report Builder 104
Chapter Summary 105
Python's Built-in Functions and High-Quality Coding Standards 106
Theoretical Foundation 106
Built-in Functions: Complete Reference 107
PEP 8: High-Quality Coding Standards 109
Implementation and Code Examples 111
Combining Built-ins with User-Defined Functions 115
The Active Learning Framework 118
Coding Challenge: Inventory Analyser 124
Chapter Summary 125
Loops and Iteration 126
Theoretical Foundation 126
Formal Syntax and Declaration 129
Implementation and Code Examples 131
The Active Learning Framework 135

- Coding Challenge: Number Guessing Game 140
- Chapter Summary 141

Python Lists 142
- Theoretical Foundation 142
- Formal Syntax and Declaration 145
- Implementation and Code Examples 146
- The Active Learning Framework 151
- Coding Challenge: Playlist Manager 156
- Chapter Summary 157

Strings as Sequences 158
- Theoretical Foundation 158
- Formal Syntax and Declaration 163
- Implementation and Code Examples 163
- The Active Learning Framework 168
- Coding Challenge: Password Strength Analyser 173
- Chapter Summary 174

Dictionaries and Tuples 175
- Theoretical Foundation 175
- Formal Syntax and Declaration 179
- Implementation and Code Examples 181
- The Active Learning Framework 185
- Coding Challenge: Contact Book 190
- Chapter Summary 191

Exception Handling 192
- Theoretical Foundation 192
- Formal Syntax and Declaration 195
- Implementation and Code Examples 196
- The Active Learning Framework 201
- Coding Challenge: Robust Student Score Importer 207
- Chapter Summary 208

Object-Oriented Programming 209
- Theoretical Foundation 209
- Formal Syntax and Declaration 212
- Implementation and Code Examples 214
- The Active Learning Framework 220
- Coding Challenge: Library Management System 227
- Chapter Summary 228

Appendix A Python Quick Reference 229
- Built-in Data Types 229

Operators........ 229
Control Flow Syntax........ 229
Key String Methods........ 230
Key List Methods........ 230
Key Dictionary Methods........ 231
f-String Format Specifiers........ 231
Essential Built-in Functions........ 231
Glossary........ 234

Chapter Overview

Ch	Chapter Title	Key Topics
Ch 01	Introduction to Programming and Python	Programming concepts, Python ecosystem, IDLE, first script, print(), comments, PEP 8 introduction
Ch 02	Fundamentals, Variables, and Data Types	Variables, assignment, int/float/str/bool, type(), conversion, naming rules, multiple assignment
Ch 03	Input, Output, and Arithmetic Operations	input(), int()/float() casting, operators, precedence, f-strings, round(), formatted output
Ch 04	Boolean Logic and Comparison Operators	True/False, comparison operators, and/or/not, truth tables, compound conditions, short-circuit evaluation
Ch 05	Python Conditionals	if/elif/else chains, nested conditionals, indentation rules, one-liner expressions
Ch 06	The Python match-case Statement	match-case syntax, literal patterns, OR patterns, guard clauses, wildcard _, comparison with if/elif
Ch 07	Functions in Python	def, parameters vs arguments, return, scope (LEGB), default arguments, *args/**kwargs, docstrings
Ch 08	Python's Built-in Functions and High-Quality Coding Standards	print/input/type/len/range/abs/round/min/max/sorted/enumerate/zip/isinstance(), complete PEP 8 guide
Ch 09	Loops and Iteration	while loop, for loop, range(), break/continue/pass, loop else, nested loops, accumulator pattern
Ch 10	Python Lists	Indexing, slicing, mutability, append/extend/insert/remove/pop/sort, enumerate(), list comprehensions
Ch 11	Strings as Sequences	Immutability, indexing/slicing, case/testing/search/replace/split/join methods, f-string format specifiers
Ch 12	Dictionaries and Tuples	Key-value pairs, get()/update()/pop(), items()/keys()/values(), dict comprehensions, tuple unpacking
Ch 13	Exception Handling	try/except/else/finally, exception types, raise, custom exceptions (class), LBYL vs EAFP
Ch 14	Object-Oriented Programming	Classes, __init__, self, instance vs class attributes, inheritance, super(), method overriding, polymorphism

CHAPTER 1

Introduction to Programming and Python

Learning Objectives

1. Define the terms programming and algorithm using precise technical language.
2. Explain what Python is and identify at least three reasons it is widely adopted in industry and academia.
3. Contrast the execution model of an interpreted language with that of a compiled language.
4. Declare and initialize variables in Python and explain how the assignment operator works.
5. Explain the purpose of comments and correctly write both single-line and multi-line comments.
6. Describe the variable independence rule and explain why reassigning one variable cannot affect another.
7. Write and execute print() statements using the sep and end keyword arguments.
8. Apply PEP 8 naming conventions and whitespace rules to produce professional-quality code.

Theoretical Foundation

Programming is the process of writing a precise, ordered set of instructions for a computer to execute. Those instructions, taken together, form an **Algorithm**. An algorithm is any finite sequence of steps designed to accomplish a defined goal. A kitchen recipe is an algorithm. A boarding process at an airport is an algorithm. When you write a program, you are translating a human-readable algorithm into a notation the machine can parse and act on.

Every programming language enforces a set of grammatical rules called its **Syntax**. Syntax governs exactly how statements must be structured. Violate the syntax, and the program cannot execute. The machine has no capacity for guessing intent.

What Python Is

Python is a **high-level, interpreted, general-purpose programming language**. High-level means Python's syntax reads close to plain English. You describe what you want to happen, and the language's runtime handles the low-level translation. Python is also **dynamically typed**, meaning you do not declare the data type of a variable before using it. Python inspects the assigned value and determines the type automatically at runtime.

Python has grown into one of the most widely deployed languages across industry and research. Libraries like TensorFlow and PyTorch power machine learning workflows. Pandas and NumPy handle large-scale data analysis. Frameworks such as Django and Flask drive web applications. These are not separate tools that happen to use Python. They are the reason Python became dominant.

How Python Runs: Interpreter vs. Compiler

Languages like C++ and Java are **compiled**. A compiler reads the entire source file and translates it into a standalone machine-language binary before a single instruction executes. If any syntax error exists anywhere in the file, compilation fails completely. Nothing runs until every line is correct.

Python uses a different model. The **Python Interpreter** reads and executes code *line by line*, working from the top of the file to the bottom. Correct lines execute immediately. The interpreter only stops when it reaches a broken statement, and it reports exactly which line failed. That immediate feedback loop makes writing and debugging Python fast.

Property	Compiled Language (C++)	Interpreted Language (Python)
Translation Unit	Entire file at once, before execution	One line at a time, in real time
Error Discovery	All errors caught before any code runs	Error surfaces at the exact failing line during execution
Dev Speed	Slower feedback; full compile needed per change	Immediate feedback; partial scripts testable during writing

The Variable Independence Rule

This rule must be understood before attempting the logic exercises. In Python, every variable is an **independent container**. When you assign a value to a variable, you are binding that specific name to that specific piece of data in memory. No other variable is involved.

Assigning a new value to variable A replaces what A holds. Variable B is completely unaffected. There is no automatic link or cascade between two variables simply because they were assigned around the same time or used together in a calculation. Each variable tracks its own value independently.

Memory Rule: Variable Independence
Rule: Assigning a new value to one variable has absolutely no effect on any other variable, regardless of how they were initialized or used together.
Example: If score = 10, and then you write score = 50, the variable score now holds 50. Any other variable that was assigned alongside score, such as lives = 3, still holds exactly 3. Python does not cascade assignments.

Formal Syntax and Declaration

Variable Declaration and Initialization

In many compiled languages, you must explicitly declare a variable's type before assigning it a value. Python collapses those two steps into one. The moment you write `variable_name = value`, the variable is **declared** and **initialized** simultaneously. The assignment operator (`=`) does not mean "equal to." It means "assign this value to this name."

Variable names must be descriptive and follow **snake_case** convention: all lowercase letters, with underscores separating words. Names like `player_score`, `total_price`, and `file_name` are correct. Single-letter names like `x` or `n` have no place outside of temporary loop counters.

```python
# Variable Declaration and Initialization
# Syntax: variable_name = value

player_score = 0          # int: declared and initialized to 0
user_name    = "Alex"      # str: assigned a string literal
item_price   = 19.99      # float: assigned a decimal value
is_active    = True       # bool: assigned a Boolean truth value
```

Comments: Documenting Your Code

A **comment** is text written inside a source file that the Python interpreter completely ignores at runtime. Comments serve one purpose: to communicate intent to a human reader. They explain *why* a piece of code exists, not just *what* it does. A line that reads `total = price * quantity` is self-evident. A comment that explains why a 7% tax rate was hardcoded, or why a specific fallback value was chosen, provides context the code itself cannot.

Python offers two comment forms. A **single-line comment** begins with the hash character (`#`). Everything following the `#` on that line is ignored. An **inline comment** places a `#` on the same line as a code statement, separated by at least two spaces. A **multi-line comment** uses triple quotes (`"""`) and is typically placed at the top of a file or function to describe its overall purpose. This is called a **docstring**.

```python
# ----------------------------------------------
# Comment Types in Python
# ----------------------------------------------

"""
This is a multi-line docstring.
It describes the purpose of this script.
The interpreter skips all of this text.
```

```
"""

# This is a single-line comment (entire line ignored)
launch_speed = 11.2  # km/s — escape velocity from Earth (inline comment)

# Bad comment (states the obvious — avoid this):
total = price + tax  # adds price and tax  <- unnecessary

# Good comment (explains the WHY, not the WHAT):
total = price + tax  # tax calculated at state rate per invoice #4421
```

The print() Function

The **print()** function is Python's primary output mechanism. It accepts one or more arguments, converts each to its string representation, and writes the result to the console. The function has four keyword parameters beyond the required value: `sep`, `end`, `file`, and `flush`. The first two alter how output is formatted.

Parameter	Default Value	What It Controls
value	(required)	The object(s) to display. Non-string objects are auto-converted using str().
sep	' ' (one space)	The string inserted between values when multiple arguments are passed.
end	'\n' (newline)	The string appended after the last value. Override this to suppress the automatic line break.
flush	False	Forces the output stream to flush immediately. Rarely needed in basic scripts.

Indentation: The Golden Rule

Python uses **indentation** to define code structure. In other languages, curly braces group statements. In Python, consistent whitespace does that work. Every line of sequential, top-level code must start at column 0. Introducing even one unintentional space before a top-level statement triggers an immediate **IndentationError**. Four spaces is the PEP 8 standard for any indented block.

Syntax Rule: Indentation

Every line of sequential code in a basic script must begin at the exact left margin. A rogue leading space on any top-level statement will cause an IndentationError and prevent the program from running. This rule becomes especially critical when writing loops and conditionals in later chapters.

Implementation and Code Examples

Example 1 — Basic String Output

The simplest complete Python program sends a text message to the console. Study the structure: `print` is the function name, the argument is a string literal in quotation marks, and the parentheses tell Python to execute the call.

```
Python

# Example 1: Basic String Output
# print() sends its argument to the console display.

print("Hello, Python Student!")
```

⚡ Quick Start: No Setup Required

Do not let environment setup delay your learning. You can execute every program in this chapter immediately at www.aymanalzaid.com/pysurgeon. Open it in your browser, type the program exactly as shown, and press Run. This is not a long-term substitute for a local environment, but it removes the setup barrier so you can start verifying your predictions today.

Expected Output

```
Hello, Python Student!
```

Example 2 — Customizing sep and end Parameters

By default, `print()` places a space between multiple arguments and adds a newline at the end. Both defaults can be overridden. Passing a custom `sep` changes the separator. Passing a custom `end` changes what follows the last value. Setting `end=' '` instead of `end='\n'` keeps the cursor on the same line, allowing the next print() call to continue on the same row.

```
Python

# Example 2: Customizing sep and end

# sep changes the separator between multiple arguments
print("Data", "Science", sep="-")    # Output: Data-Science
```

```
# end suppresses the default newline — keeps cursor on same line
print("Loading", end="... ")
print("Complete!")          # Output: Loading... Complete!
```

Expected Output

```
Data-Science
Loading... Complete!
```

Example 3 — String Concatenation vs. Integer Addition

Python decides what an operator does based entirely on the data types of its operands. The + symbol has two completely different behaviors depending on what sits on either side of it.

When + operates on two **strings**, it joins them side-by-side. This is **string concatenation**. When + operates on two **integers**, it performs arithmetic addition. The characters "10" and "20" written inside quotation marks are text data, not numeric quantities.

```
Python
# Example 3: Type-Dependent Operator Behavior

# Case A: string operands — + concatenates characters
print("10" + "20")     # Output: 1020  (text joined, not added)

# Case B: integer operands — + performs arithmetic
print(10 + 20)         # Output: 30  (numeric sum computed)
```

Expression	Operand Type	Operator Behavior	Result
"10" + "20"	str + str	Concatenation — characters joined left-to-right	"1020"
10 + 20	int + int	Arithmetic addition — values summed numerically	30

Example 4 — Variable Mutation and Reassignment

This example demonstrates how a variable's stored value is replaced by a subsequent assignment. The interpreter updates its internal record of that variable at the exact line the assignment executes. Previous values are overwritten and gone.

```python
# Example 4: Variable Initialization and Sequential Reassignment

# Step 1: Initialize the variable with an integer value of 0
player_score = 0
print(player_score)  # Output: 0

# Step 2: Mutate — assign a completely new value to the same variable
player_score = 15  # old value (0) is permanently replaced
print(player_score)  # Output: 15

# Step 3: A second variable is completely unaffected by Step 2
player_lives  = 3   # independent — changing score does NOT change lives
print(player_lives)   # Output: 3
```

Expected Output
0
15
3

Example 5 — Division Operators: Three Different Results

Python offers three division operators, each returning a different type of result. True division (/) always returns a float. Floor division (//) returns only the integer portion of the quotient, discarding any remainder. The modulo operator (%) returns only the remainder.

```python
# Example 5: All Three Division Operators

numerator   = 10  # the number being divided
denominator = 4   # the number we divide by

# / always returns float — even 10/2 returns 5.0, not 5
```

```
print(numerator / denominator)    # Output: 2.5

# // returns the integer quotient only — .5 is discarded
print(numerator // denominator)   # Output: 2

# % returns only the remainder: 10 = (4 * 2) + 2, so remainder is 2
print(numerator % denominator)    # Output: 2
```

Expected Output
2.5
2
2

Code Quality and Professional Standards

Writing code that runs is only the first step. Professional software engineering holds a higher standard. Code must be readable by anyone who opens it, maintainable across months of changes, and debuggable under pressure. These are not cosmetic concerns. They are functional requirements in any collaborative development environment.

Meaningful Naming Conventions

Python follows the **snake_case** convention for all variable and function names. Every word is lowercase. Words are separated by underscores. The name must describe the data it holds. A variable named `n` tells the reader nothing. A variable named `total_items_in_cart` is immediately understood by any developer reading the code.

Type	Convention	Correct Example	Incorrect Example
Variables	lowercase_snake_case	player_score, item_count	PlayerScore, itemCount, x
Constants	ALL_CAPS_SNAKE_CASE	MAX_RETRIES, PI_VALUE	maxRetries, pi
Functions	lowercase_snake_case	calculate_total()	CalculateTotal(), calcT()

PEP 8: The Python Style Standard

PEP 8 is the official Python style guide. It governs whitespace, naming, line length, and comment formatting. Violating PEP 8 does not break the program. It signals poor engineering discipline and makes code harder to maintain. The key rules for this chapter are straightforward. Place one space on both sides of the = operator. Place one space on both sides of arithmetic operators. Never place unnecessary spaces inside parentheses. Limit lines to 79 characters.

The Active Learning Framework

The three pillars below apply the theory from this chapter through progressive challenge exercises. Work through each one in sequence.

Pillar	Activity Type	What You Do	Cognitive Skill Targeted
P1 Logic	Logic Exercises	Trace variables and step through interpreter execution one line at a time.	Builds an accurate mental model of Python memory allocation and mutation.
P2 Puzzle	Mysterious Output	Predict the output of tricky edge-case scripts before executing them.	Exposes hidden edge cases and sharpens precision code-tracing.
P3 Audit	Code Audits	Diagnose and refactor poorly written scripts to PEP 8 standards.	Trains professional discipline in clean code architecture and style.

Pillar 1 — Logic Exercise: Interpreter Trace

Tracing the interpreter means stepping through a script exactly as Python's runtime would. Read each line in order. When a variable is assigned, record its new value in the table. When a print() call is reached, write down exactly what it will display on the console. Do not skip lines. Do not run the code first.

Apply three rules during the trace. **Rule 1:** Assigning a new value to a variable replaces the old value permanently. The previous value is gone. **Rule 2:** The `str()` function converts a non-string value into its text representation so it can be joined with strings using +. **Rule 3:** Variables are independent. Reassigning one variable has no effect on any other.

PILLAR 1 Logic Exercise

Instructions: Read the script one line at a time. Complete the Execution Trace Table. Record the state of each variable and any console output after every statement. Do not run the code.

Python

```python
# Pillar 1: Interpreter Trace Exercise

language_name = "Python"
```

```
version_number = 3
print(language_name + " version: " + str(version_number))
language_name = "MicroPython"
print(language_name)
```

Execution Trace Table

Statement Executed	language_name	version_number	Console Output
language_name = "Python"	"Python"	—	—
version_number = 3	"Python"	3	—
print(language_name + ...)	"Python"	3	? ← fill in
language_name = "MicroPython"	"MicroPython"	3	—
print(language_name)	"MicroPython"	3	? ← fill in

Challenge Questions: Fill in both missing console outputs. What does str(version_number) produce and why is it needed? Why does reassigning language_name on line 4 leave version_number completely unchanged?

Pillar 2 — Mysterious Output Puzzles: Predict Before You Run

Each puzzle below tests a specific rule covered in this chapter. Read the code carefully. Think through what each operator and function call will produce. Record your prediction for every print() statement. Only after committing to all predictions should, you run the code to verify.

PILLAR 2 Mysterious Output Puzzles

Instructions: Predict every line of output for each puzzle before running any of them. Record your predictions. Then execute the code and compare your results.

Puzzle 1.1 — The Double Agent Operator

Pay close attention to the quotation marks. `value_a` and `value_b` are assigned twice, first as strings, then as integers. Track every reassignment and decide what type the + operator is working with at each print() call.

```python
# Puzzle 1.1: The Double Agent Operator

value_a = "40"
value_b = "20"
```

```
result_1 = value_a + value_b

value_a = 40
value_b = 20
result_2 = value_a + value_b

print(result_1)
print(result_2)
```

Questions: What is the exact console output for both print statements? How does the data type of the operands change the behavior of the + operator between result_1 and result_2?

Puzzle 1.2 — The Hidden Boundary

Read the second print statement closely. Note where the inline comment begins. The characters following the # are ignored by the interpreter. Does that change what the second print() call displays?

```python
# Puzzle 1.2: The Hidden Boundary

items  = 11
crates = 4

print(items / crates)
print(items // crates)  # print(items)
print(items % crates)
```

Questions: What does the second print statement actually display? Why does the first print statement return a decimal even though both starting variables are whole integers?

Puzzle 1.3 — Overriding the Stream Defaults

Track how changing `sep` and `end` alters the final display. Count how many physical lines of text will appear on the console.

```python
# Puzzle 1.3: Overriding the Stream Defaults

label = "Error"
code  = 404
```

```python
print(label, code, sep=":")
print("Analyzing", end="... ")
print("System Clear")
```

Questions: How many lines of text will appear on the console? What happened to the default space separator in the first call? What happened to the default line break in the second call?

Puzzle 1.4 — The Rogue Space Trap

Analyze the script below. Before predicting output, decide whether the script will execute successfully or trigger an error. Apply the indentation rule from the Formal Syntax section.

```python
# Puzzle 1.4: The Rogue Space Trap

message = "Initializing setup"
  print(message)
```

Questions: Will this script execute from top to bottom? If not, what error will Python raise and on which line? What specific foundational syntax rule did this script violate?

Pillar 3 — Code Audit: Refactor to PEP 8

PEP 8 compliance is not cosmetic. In professional environments, code that violates the style guide is returned for revision before it is accepted into a codebase. The audit below follows a three-step process: read the non-compliant script and identify every violation, record each violation in the table with its specific PEP 8 rule, then rewrite the entire script to production standards.

🛠 PILLAR 3 Code Audit — Refactor to PEP 8

Instructions: Study the non-compliant script. Identify every PEP 8 violation and record it in the audit table. Then rewrite the entire script to production standards in your own workspace.

Non-Compliant Script

```python
# bad script
x="hello"
```

```
Y=42
print( x)
print(Y  )
z=x+"world"
print(z)
```

Violation Audit Table

#	Violation Found	PEP 8 Rule Broken	Corrected Pattern
1	x="hello" (no spaces around =)	E225: Missing whitespace around operator	x = "hello"
2	Variable Y uses uppercase	E741 / Convention: Variables should be lowercase_snake_case	count = 42
3	print(x) has extra space after (	E201: Whitespace after parenthesis	print(x)
4	print(Y) has trailing spaces	W291 / E202: Trailing whitespace	print(count)
5	No module-level docstring or descriptive comment	Convention: Scripts should have a descriptive header comment	Add """...""" or # header

Production-Quality Refactored Script

```python
# ---------------------------------------------------
# Module  : chapter_01_audit_solution.py
# Purpose : Demonstrates PEP 8 compliant variable
#           declaration and clean print() usage.
# Author  : Ayman Alzaid
# ---------------------------------------------------

greeting     = "hello"    # descriptive lowercase name (PEP 8)
count         = 42        # spaces around = operator (E225)

print(greeting)              # no whitespace inside parentheses (E201)
print(count)                 # no trailing spaces (E202)

full_message = greeting + " world"    # spaces around + operator (E225)
print(full_message)
```

Coding Challenge: Final Programming Task

Chapter 1 Coding Challenge

Objective: Write a complete, PEP 8 compliant Python script that demonstrates mastery of this chapter. Every requirement below must be satisfied in your submitted solution.

- Open with a professional header comment block: module name, author (your name), date, and a one-sentence description of what the program does.
- Declare four variables representing real personal data: full name (str), age (int), GPA (float), and enrolled status (bool). Use descriptive snake_case names.
- Write single-line comments explaining the purpose of at least two of your four variables.
- Use print() with the sep parameter to display at least two values separated by a custom character.
- Use print() with the end parameter to print two consecutive statements on the same line.
- Perform and display the result of all three division operators (/, //, %) using your age value.
- Demonstrate string concatenation by combining your name with a greeting message.

Chapter Summary

Concept	Key Takeaway
Programming	Writing precise algorithmic instructions for a computer to parse and execute.
Algorithm	A finite, ordered sequence of steps designed to accomplish a defined computational goal.
Syntax	The grammatical rules of a language. Any violation produces an immediate parse error.
Python vs. Compiled	Python executes line by line at runtime. Compiled languages translate the entire file before execution begins.
Variable Independence	Assigning a value to one variable has no effect on any other variable, regardless of context.
Initialization	In Python, declaration and initialization happen simultaneously at the moment of assignment.
Comments (#)	Non-executable text written for human readers. Single-line uses #, multi-line uses triple quotes.
print()	Python's primary output function. Converts arguments to strings and writes them to the console.
sep and end	Keyword arguments that override print()'s default space separator and newline terminator.
Type-Dependent +	The + operator concatenates strings and adds integers. Behavior is determined by operand type.
Division Operators	/ returns float. // returns integer quotient. % returns the remainder.
PEP 8	The official Python style guide. Defines whitespace rules, naming conventions, and comment standards.

CHAPTER 2

Fundamentals, Variables, and Data Types

Learning Objectives

1. Explain how Python stores data in memory and describe the difference between mutable and immutable objects.
2. Declare and initialize variables of all four core primitive data types: int, float, str, and bool.
3. Use the type() function to inspect the data type of any variable at runtime.
4. Apply augmented assignment operators (+=, -=, *=, /=) to update variable values efficiently.
5. Perform explicit type conversion between int, float, and str using Python's built-in casting functions.
6. Predict which inputs will raise a ValueError during type casting and explain why.
7. Identify and correct type mismatch errors that occur when mixing incompatible data types in expressions.
8. Write production-quality variable declarations following PEP 8 naming and whitespace conventions.

Theoretical Foundation

Variables as Memory Labels

A **variable** is a named reference to a location in the computer's memory. The name itself holds no data. It is a label, like a tag tied to a box on a warehouse shelf. The box holds the actual data. The tag tells you where to find it. When you write `player_score = 100`, Python reserves a memory location to hold the integer `100`, and binds the name `player_score` to that location. From that point forward, anywhere `player_score` appears in the script, the interpreter knows exactly which shelf to look at.

The assignment operator (`=`) does not test equality. It performs **binding**. The interpreter evaluates whatever is on the right side first, produces a value, stores it in memory, and then attaches the name on the left side to it. That direction matters. The right side is always evaluated first.

Dynamic Typing: What It Actually Means

Python is a **dynamically typed** language. In statically typed languages like C++ or Java, you must declare the type of a variable before assigning it a value, and that type is locked for the lifetime of the variable. Python makes no such requirement. At the moment you assign a value, the interpreter inspects that value and determines its type automatically at runtime. You can later reassign the same variable name to a completely different type without any explicit conversion.

This flexibility is powerful and must be handled with discipline. A variable that holds an integer early in a script can hold a string later. The interpreter will not stop you. But if code elsewhere assumes the variable is still an integer and attempts arithmetic, a type mismatch error will surface. Disciplined naming and consistent usage are the tools that prevent this class of bug.

Key Distinction: Dynamic vs. Static Typing
Static Typing (C++, Java): int score = 100; — the type is locked. Assigning a string to score later causes a compile error.
Dynamic Typing (Python): score = 100 — the type is inferred. score = "Error" later is legal. You carry the responsibility for consistency.

The Four Core Primitive Data Types

Python has four core data types that cover the vast majority of everyday values. Every value you work with in this chapter belongs to one of these four categories. Study the table below, paying close attention to the specific formatting rules for each type.

Data Type	Python Keyword	Declaration Example	Key Rule
Integer	int	score = 100	Whole numbers only. No decimal point. Can be positive, negative, or zero.
Float	float	price = 19.95	Numbers with a decimal point. Use for measurements and currency values.
String	str	username = "Alex"	Any sequence of characters. Must be enclosed in matching quotation marks.
Boolean	bool	is_active = True	Exactly two values only: True or False. Capitalized. No quotation marks.

Memory and Immutability

All four primitive types are **immutable**. This is one of Python's most important architectural decisions. Immutability means the value stored at a given memory address cannot be altered after it is created. When you appear to "change" an integer variable, you are not modifying the original object. Python creates a completely new object at a new memory address, stores the new value there, and moves the variable label to point at the new location. The original object is abandoned and eventually cleaned up by Python's garbage collector.

This has a direct consequence for **strings**. A string cannot be changed in place. You cannot replace a single character inside an existing string. Any operation that appears to modify a string, such as adding characters to it, produces a brand-new string object. The old one is discarded. Attempting to directly assign a value to an index position inside a string will raise a **TypeError** immediately.

Figure 2.1 — How Immutable Reassignment Works in Memory

The diagram below shows what actually happens at the memory level when you reassign an integer variable. No existing object is modified. A new one is created and the label moves.

Step 1: Initial Assignment	→	Step 2: Reassignment	→	Step 3: New Object Created
score = 100	→	score = 200	→	score → NEW 200 (new obj)
Memory holds 100	→	*Python cannot modify 100*	→	*Creates fresh object: 200*

Augmented Assignment Operators

When updating the value of an existing variable, Python provides **augmented assignment operators** that combine an arithmetic operation with the reassignment step into a single, readable expression. The operator += reads as "take the current value, add this amount to it, and rebind the result to the same name." Every standard arithmetic operator has an augmented form.

Augmented Operator	Equivalent Longform	Reads As
score += 10	score = score + 10	"Add 10 to score"
score -= 5	score = score - 5	"Subtract 5 from score"
score *= 2	score = score * 2	"Multiply score by 2"
score /= 4	score = score / 4	"Divide score by 4 (returns float)"
score //= 3	score = score // 3	"Floor-divide score by 3 (returns int)"
score %= 7	score = score % 7	"Set score to the remainder of score divided by 7"

The type() Function

Python provides a built-in function called **type()** that returns the exact data type of any value or variable. The output is a type object displayed in the format <class 'typename'>. Passing a variable name into type() is the fastest way to verify what Python is actually storing. This is especially useful during debugging, when a variable may have been reassigned to an unexpected type somewhere earlier in the script.

Formal Syntax and Declaration

Type Conversion: Casting Between Types

Python provides three built-in casting functions for converting between the core types: `int()`, `float()`, and `str()`. Casting does not modify the original variable. It produces a new object of the target type. The original variable remains unchanged unless you explicitly rebind it.

Function	Converts To	Valid Input Example	Result
int("42")	Integer	A string of digit characters	42
int(3.9)	Integer	A float value	3 (truncates, does NOT round)
float("3.14")	Float	A string of a decimal number	3.14
float(5)	Float	An integer	5.0
str(100)	String	Any number	"100"
str(True)	String	A boolean	"True"

The ValueError: When Casting Fails

Casting fails when the input value is logically incompatible with the target type. Passing the word `"Offline"` to `int()` produces an immediate **ValueError** because the interpreter cannot construct an integer from non-numeric characters. The program stops at that line. Nothing after it executes.

ValueError: Common Casting Failures
Fails: `int("Offline")` — non-numeric characters cannot become an integer.
Fails: `int("7.5")` — int() does not accept decimal strings. Use float() first, then int().
Fails: `float("hello")` — no numeric representation exists for alphabetic text.
Safe Pattern: `int(float("7.5"))` — convert to float first, then truncate to int.

Type Mismatch Errors

A **TypeError** occurs when an operator receives operands of incompatible types. The clearest example is adding a string and an integer with the + operator. Python will not guess your intent or attempt automatic conversion. The script stops and reports the mismatch precisely.

The fix is always explicit. If you need to combine a number with a string for display, wrap the number in `str()`. If you need to perform arithmetic on a value that arrived as a string, wrap it in `int()` or `float()` first. Never rely on Python to perform implicit cross-type conversions in arithmetic or concatenation contexts.

Implementation and Code Examples

Example 1 — Declaring All Four Data Types

Study the initialization pattern for each type. Notice the spacing around the assignment operator, the aligned formatting for readability, and the inline comments explaining the purpose of each variable.

```python
# Example 1: Declaring All Four Core Primitive Data Types
# Each variable stores a different kind of data in memory.

current_score   = 0          # int: whole number, starts at zero
item_price      = 24.99      # float: decimal value for currency
player_username = "Alex"     # str: text enclosed in double quotes
is_logged_in    = True       # bool: True or False — capitalized, no quotes

# Displaying all four variables on the console
print(current_score)
print(item_price)
print(player_username)
print(is_logged_in)
```

Expected Output

```
0
24.99
Alex
True
```

Example 2 — Using type() to Inspect Variables

The `type()` function wraps around any variable or value and returns its exact type as a class object. This is how you verify what the interpreter is actually storing, especially after a reassignment or a casting operation.

```python
# Example 2: Inspecting Data Types with type()
```

```
score     = 100
price     = 9.99
username  = "Alex"
is_ready  = False

# type() returns the class of the value passed to it
print(type(score))      # Output: <class 'int'>
print(type(price))      # Output: <class 'float'>
print(type(username))   # Output: <class 'str'>
print(type(is_ready))   # Output: <class 'bool'>
```

Expected Output

```
<class 'int'>
<class 'float'>
<class 'str'>
<class 'bool'>
```

Example 3 — Augmented Assignment Operators in Action

Read each augmented assignment line carefully and trace what happens to the variable at each step. Pay attention to the floor division operator — it returns an integer, which changes the type of the variable from what it was before.

```python
# Example 3: Augmented Assignment Operators
# Each operator updates the variable using its current value.

player_score = 50       # initialize at 50
print(player_score)       # Output: 50

player_score += 20      # 50 + 20 = 70
print(player_score)       # Output: 70

player_score -= 5       # 70 - 5 = 65
print(player_score)       # Output: 65

player_score *= 2       # 65 * 2 = 130
print(player_score)       # Output: 130

player_score //= 3      # 130 // 3 = 43 (integer quotient)
```

```
print(player_score)         # Output: 43
```

Expected Output
50
70
65
130
43

Example 4 — Explicit Type Conversion (Casting)

Study how each casting function transforms the data. Notice particularly that `int(3.9)` does not round to 4. It truncates toward zero, producing 3. Rounding and truncation are not the same operation.

```python
# Example 4: Explicit Type Conversion

# Converting a string to an integer for arithmetic
text_value  = "42"            # currently a string
int_value   = int(text_value)     # cast to int: 42
print(int_value + 8)         # Output: 50

# Converting a float to int TRUNCATES (does not round)
decimal_val = 3.9             # float
print(int(decimal_val))       # Output: 3  (NOT 4)

# Converting a number to a string for safe concatenation
age          = 25
message       = "Age: " + str(age)  # str() needed before concatenation
print(message)                # Output: Age: 25

# Safe two-step pattern: string decimal → float → int
raw_input   = "7.5"
safe_int    = int(float(raw_input))  # Output: 7
print(safe_int)
```

Expected Output
50
3
Age: 25
7

Example 5 — Type Mismatch and the Correct Fix

The script below demonstrates the exact point at which a **TypeError** occurs when incompatible types are combined. Read the failing version first, understand exactly which line causes the crash and why, then study the corrected version.

```python
# Example 5: TypeError — Adding a String and an Integer

# FAILING VERSION
error_code    = 404           # int
error_label  = "Error: "       # str

# This line crashes: cannot concatenate str and int
# print(error_label + error_code)   <-- TypeError here

# CORRECTED VERSION — cast the int to str before joining
full_message = error_label + str(error_code)
print(full_message)         # Output: Error: 404
```

Expected Output
Error: 404

The Active Learning Framework

The three pillars below apply this chapter's concepts through progressive challenge exercises. Pillar 1 tests your ability to trace memory state line by line. Pillar 2 pushes your ability to predict subtle output differences before running code. Pillar 3 asks you to identify design violations and reconstruct the script to professional standards. Work through all three in sequence.

Pillar	Activity Type	What You Do	Cognitive Skill Targeted
P1 Logic	Logic Exercises	Trace variables and step through interpreter execution one line at a time.	Builds an accurate mental model of Python memory allocation and mutation.
P2 Puzzle	Mysterious Output	Predict the output of tricky edge-case scripts before executing them.	Exposes hidden edge cases and sharpens precision code-tracing.
P3 Audit	Code Audits	Diagnose and refactor poorly written scripts to PEP 8 standards.	Trains professional discipline in clean code architecture and style.

Pillar 1 — Logic Exercise: Memory Box Tracking

This exercise tests your understanding of augmented assignment, variable independence, and immutability. Trace the script exactly as the interpreter would. Record the value stored in each variable after every statement executes. Apply these three rules during your trace.

Rule 1: An augmented assignment like `box_alpha += box_beta` evaluates the right side first using the *current* values of both variables. It does NOT create a live link. If `box_beta` changes afterward, `box_alpha` is not affected.

Rule 2: Variable reassignment is immediate. The old value is gone the moment the new assignment executes.

Rule 3: Variables are independent containers. Modifying one never cascades to another unless the code explicitly sets up that dependency.

PILLAR 1 Logic Exercise

Instructions: Step through the script one line at a time. Fill in the Execution Trace Table completely. Record the exact values of box_alpha, box_beta, and any console output after every statement. Do not run the code first.

Python

```python
# Pillar 1: Memory Box Tracking — Trace Exercise

box_alpha  = 10
box_beta   = 20
box_alpha  += box_beta   # augmented assignment uses CURRENT value of box_beta
box_beta   = 30       # reassignment — does NOT reach back into box_alpha
print(box_alpha)
```

```
print(box_beta)
print(type(box_alpha))
```

Execution Trace Table

Statement Executed	box_alpha	box_beta	Console Output
box_alpha = 10	10	—	—
box_beta = 20	10	20	—
box_alpha += box_beta	? ← compute	20	—
box_beta = 30	?	30	—
print(box_alpha)	?	30	? ← fill in
print(box_beta)	?	30	? ← fill in
print(type(box_alpha))	?	30	? ← fill in

Challenge Questions: What does box_alpha hold after line 3 executes? When box_beta is reassigned to 30 on line 4, why does box_alpha not change? What does type(box_alpha) return and why?

Pillar 2 — Mysterious Output Puzzles: Predict Before You Run

Each puzzle tests a specific edge case covered in this chapter. Type mismatch, unexpected operator behavior on non-numeric types, truncation versus rounding, and boolean arithmetic all appear below. Read each script carefully. Commit to a prediction for every print() statement. Record it in writing before executing anything.

PILLAR 2 Mysterious Output Puzzles

Instructions: For each puzzle, predict every line of output before running the code. Record your predictions first, then verify by executing and compare your results against the actual output.

Puzzle 2.1 — The String Multiplier

The * operator does not always perform arithmetic. When one operand is a string and the other is an integer, the operator changes its behavior entirely. Predict both outputs and explain the difference between them.

```
Python

# Puzzle 2.1: The String Multiplier

text_factor  = "7"
```

```
math_factor  = 3

# Case A: string * int – what does Python produce?
result_1  = text_factor * math_factor

# Case B: int * int – straightforward arithmetic
result_2  = int(text_factor) * math_factor

print(result_1)
print(result_2)
print(type(result_1))
```

Questions: What does result_1 hold? Is it a number or text? Why? What happens if you change the code to `int("7.5") * 3` — does Python accept that, and if not, what should you write instead?

Puzzle 2.2 — The Truncation Trap

Recall that `int()` truncates toward zero. It does not round. Predict all four outputs before running and explain the difference between truncation and rounding for both positive and negative inputs.

```python
# Puzzle 2.2: The Truncation Trap

print(int(3.9))      # Truncates 3.9 – predict carefully
print(int(3.1))      # Truncates 3.1 – predict carefully
print(int(-2.9))     # Negative truncation – which direction?
print(int(float("7.5")))  # Two-step safe cast
```

Questions: Do int(3.9) and int(3.1) produce different results? What does int(-2.9) return — is it -2 or -3? Why does int() move toward zero and not toward the nearest whole number?

Puzzle 2.3 — Boolean Arithmetic

In Python, `True` has an integer value of 1 and `False` has a value of 0. This means boolean values can participate in arithmetic expressions. Predict every output and explain why the results are what they are.

```python
# Puzzle 2.3: Boolean Arithmetic

print(True + True)          # What is True + True?
```

```
print(True + False)          # What is True + False?
print(False * 100)          # What is False * 100?
print(type(True + 1))       # What type does True + 1 produce?
```

Questions: What integer values do True and False hold? What type does True + 1 produce? How does knowing this change the way you think about boolean comparisons in later chapters?

Puzzle 2.4 — The Data Type Swap

Track every type change in the variable below. The same name is reassigned to three different types across the script. Predict the output and the type at each print() call.

```
# Puzzle 2.4: The Data Type Swap

container  = 100
print(type(container))

container  = str(container)  # rebind to a new type
print(type(container))
print(container + "!")

container  = float(container)  # cast str to float
print(type(container))
print(container + 0.5)
```

Questions: List the type of container at each print(type()) call in order. What does container + "!" produce? What does float(container) do — and at that point, what string is inside container?

Pillar 3 — Code Audit: Reassignment and Type Safety

The script below executes without a SyntaxError, but it violates two professional software engineering principles. First, it reuses a single descriptive variable name for completely unrelated types of data, which is a naming discipline failure. Second, it attempts to combine a string and an integer with the + operator, which crashes at runtime with a TypeError. These are not theoretical problems. In a production codebase, this pattern causes intermittent failures that are difficult to reproduce and trace.

Read the script. Identify the two violations. Record each in the audit table. Then rewrite the entire script to production standards, giving each distinct value its own descriptively named variable and applying explicit casting where values must be combined.

🛠 PILLAR 3 Code Audit — Type Safety and Naming Standards

Instructions: Identify every violation in the script below. Record each one in the audit table. Then rewrite the complete script to production standards, correcting all issues.

Non-Compliant Script

```python
# audit script

data_holder = 45
print(data_holder + 5)

# Same variable name reused for a completely different type
data_holder = "Offline"
print(data_holder + 5)    # TypeError — crashes here
```

Violation Audit Table

#	Violation Found	Engineering Rule Broken	Corrected Approach
1	data_holder reused for two unrelated types (int, then str)	Naming discipline: each distinct value must have its own descriptive variable name.	Use inventory_count = 45 and connection_status = "Offline" separately.
2	data_holder + 5 after reassignment to str causes TypeError	Type safety: never mix incompatible types with + operator without explicit casting.	Use str(inventory_count) or int/float casting where values must combine.
3	data_holder has no descriptive intent	PEP 8 naming: variable names must reveal their purpose and content.	inventory_count, connection_status — clear and unambiguous.

Production-Quality Refactored Script

```python
# --------------------------------------------------
# Module  : chapter_02_audit_solution.py
# Purpose : Demonstrates type-safe variable design
#           and PEP 8 compliant naming conventions.
# Author  : Ayman Alzaid
# --------------------------------------------------

# Two distinct values — two distinct, descriptive variable names
```

```
inventory_count    = 45          # int: number of items in stock
connection_status  = "Offline"     # str: current system status

# Safe arithmetic — both operands are integers
print(inventory_count + 5)       # Output: 50

# Safe string output — no type mixing attempted
print(connection_status)            # Output: Offline

# If combining is needed: explicit casting
status_report      = "Count: " + str(inventory_count)
print(status_report)               # Output: Count: 45
```

Coding Challenge: Employee Profile Builder

Chapter 2 Coding Challenge

Objective: Build a complete employee profile script that demonstrates mastery of all four data types, type inspection, augmented assignment, and explicit casting. Every requirement below must appear in your submitted code.

- Open with a PEP 8 compliant header comment block: module name, author, date, and a one-sentence description.
- Declare four variables representing an employee record: full name (str), hourly rate (float), years employed (int), and active status (bool). Use descriptive snake_case names.
- Write single-line comments for at least three of your four variables explaining what each one stores.
- Use type() to print the data type of each variable immediately after declaring it.
- Use an augmented assignment operator to increment years_employed by 1, then print the updated value.
- Calculate gross weekly pay (hourly_rate * 40) and store the result in a new variable. Print it.
- Build and print a formatted status string by combining at least two variables using str() casting.

Chapter Summary

Concept	Key Takeaway
Variables as Labels	A variable name is a reference to a memory location. It does not store data directly — it points to it.
Dynamic Typing	Python infers data types at runtime. The same variable name can hold different types at different points in a script.
Immutability	Integers, floats, strings, and booleans cannot be modified in place. Reassignment creates a new object.
int	Whole numbers only. No decimal point. Positive, negative, or zero.
float	Numbers with a decimal point. Always returned by the / operator.
str	A sequence of characters enclosed in matching quotation marks. Cannot be modified in place.
bool	Exactly two values: True or False. Capitalized. No quotation marks. Holds integer values 1 and 0.
type()	Returns the data type of any variable or value as a class object.
Augmented Assignment	+=, -=, *=, /=, //=, %= combine an operation and reassignment into one readable expression.
int() / float() / str()	Built-in casting functions. int() truncates toward zero — it does not round.
ValueError	Raised when casting receives logically incompatible input, such as int("Offline").
TypeError	Raised when an operator receives incompatible types, such as a string + an integer.

CHAPTER 3

Input, Output, and Arithmetic Operations

Learning Objectives

1. Use the input() function to collect data from a user at runtime and store it in a variable.
2. Explain why input() always returns a string and apply correct type casting before performing arithmetic.
3. Write clear, descriptive input prompts that guide the user on exactly what format to enter.
4. Apply all seven arithmetic operators to user-supplied values and display computed results.
5. Use f-strings to format output that combines static text, variables, and computed expressions cleanly.
6. Use the round() function to control the number of decimal places in a computed result.
7. Predict the exact crash point and error type when a user enters unexpected input that breaks casting.
8. Build a complete multi-step calculation program that collects inputs, computes results, and displays formatted output.

Theoretical Foundation

Making Programs Interactive: The input() Function

Every program written in the previous two chapters worked with values the programmer typed directly into the source file. Those values are fixed before the program runs and identical every time. Real software does not work this way. A payroll calculator that only ever computes one hardcoded salary is useless.

The **input()** function breaks that limitation. It pauses execution, displays a message to the user, and waits. The user types something and presses Enter. The function captures whatever was typed and returns it as a value the script can store and act on. That exchange is the foundation of interactive software.

The Critical Rule: input() Always Returns a String

The **input()** function has one fixed return type: **str**. It does not matter what the user types. The user can type 42, 3.14, or True. The function returns a string every time. The characters the user typed are wrapped in quotation marks and handed back as text data.

If you ask a user for their age and immediately try to divide it by 2, the program crashes with a **TypeError**. You cannot divide a string. The cast must happen between the input() call and the arithmetic. This is a structural requirement of every program that collects numbers from users.

Figure 3.1 -- The Four-Step Journey from Keyboard to Calculation

Every numeric input passes through four stages before it can be used in arithmetic. The diagram below shows what happens at each stage when a user enters 25.

Step 1		Step 2		Step 3		Step 4
User Types 25	>>	input() Returns "25"	>>	int("25") Casts to 25	>>	Arithmetic 25 + 5 = 30
Keyboard entry		*Always a string*		*Now an integer*		*Safe to compute*

Writing Effective Prompts

The string passed to `input()` is the prompt. Three rules govern good prompt design: be specific about the value expected, include format guidance for decimal inputs, and end the prompt string with a trailing space to separate it visually from the user's cursor.

Rule	Weak Prompt	Strong Prompt
Be specific	input("Enter number: ")	input("Enter your age in whole years: ")
Include format hint	input("Enter price: ")	input("Enter item price (e.g. 19.99): ")
Trailing space	input("Enter name:")	input("Enter your full name: ")

Output Formatting with f-Strings

An **f-string** is a string literal prefixed with the letter `f` immediately before the opening quotation mark. Inside the string, any expression wrapped in curly braces `{...}` is evaluated at runtime and its result is inserted directly into the output. No `str()` calls, no + operators chaining segments together.

f-String Syntax Reference
Basic variable insertion: `f"Hello, {name}!"`
Inline expression: `f"Total: {price * quantity}"`
Decimal formatting: `f"Result: {value:.2f}"` -- 2 decimal places.

Function call inside: `f"Rounded: {round(value, 3)}"`

Arithmetic Operators: Complete Reference

Operator	Name	Example	Result	Notes
+	Addition	cost + tax	sum	Concatenates strings -- never mix types.
-	Subtraction	paid - total	difference	Negative results are valid.
*	Multiplication	length * width	product	str * int repeats the string.
/	True Division	distance / time	float always	10 / 2 returns 5.0 not 5.
//	Floor Division	items // per_box	int quotient	Discards the decimal part.
%	Modulo	items % per_box	int remainder	Returns remainder only.
**	Exponentiation	side ** 2	power result	2 ** 10 returns 1024.

Formal Syntax and Declaration

input() Syntax

```python
# input() -- Formal Syntax Patterns

# Pattern 1: String input -- no cast needed
name = input("Enter your name: ")

# Pattern 2: Integer input -- wrap input() inside int()
age  = int(input("Enter your age: "))

# Pattern 3: Float input -- wrap input() inside float()
price = float(input("Enter price (e.g. 9.99): "))
```

f-String Syntax

```python
# f-String -- Formal Syntax Examples

name  = "Alex"
score = 95
print(f"Player {name} scored {score} points.")

# Inline expression
print(f"Double: {score * 2}")

# Format specifier: :.2f = exactly 2 decimal places
price = 7.333333
print(f"Price: ${price:.2f}")
```

Expected Output

```
Player Alex scored 95 points.
Double: 190
Price: $7.33
```

Implementation and Code Examples

Example 1 -- Basic String Input

The simplest `input()` call collects a name. No casting needed -- the program uses the value as text throughout. Notice the trailing space inside the prompt string.

```python
# Example 1: Collecting a Name and Greeting the User

user_name = input("Enter your full name: ")
print(f"Welcome, {user_name}! Your profile has been created.")
```

Expected Output

```
Enter your full name: Alex
Welcome, Alex! Your profile has been created.
```

Example 2 -- Integer Input and Arithmetic

The `input()` call is wrapped immediately in `int()`. The result is an integer from the moment it is stored. No separate cast is needed when arithmetic runs.

```python
# Example 2: Integer Input and Arithmetic

age = int(input("Enter your age in whole years: "))

birth_year   = 2026 - age
years_to_100 = 100 - age

print(f"Estimated birth year: {birth_year}")
print(f"Years until 100: {years_to_100}")
```

Expected Output

```
Enter your age in whole years: 22
Estimated birth year: 2003
Years until 100: 78
```

Example 3 -- Float Input and Formatted Output

The `:.2f` specifier inside the curly braces formats a float to exactly 2 decimal places. Note how the specifier sits after a colon, separated from the variable name.

```python
# Example 3: Float Input, Arithmetic, and Formatted Output

item_price = float(input("Enter item price (e.g. 9.99): "))
quantity   = int(input("Enter quantity: "))
```

```
subtotal   = item_price * quantity
tax_amount = subtotal * 0.08   # 8% tax rate
total_due  = subtotal + tax_amount

print(f"Subtotal:  ${subtotal:.2f}")
print(f"Tax (8%): ${tax_amount:.2f}")
print(f"Total:    ${total_due:.2f}")
```

Expected Output

```
Enter item price (e.g. 9.99): 12.50
Enter quantity: 3
Subtotal:  $37.50
Tax (8%): $3.00
Total:    $40.50
```

Example 4 -- All Seven Operators

This example collects two numbers and applies every arithmetic operator, displaying each result with a descriptive label. This is the foundation of any calculator program.

```
Python
# Example 4: All Seven Arithmetic Operators

num_a = float(input("Enter first number: "))
num_b = float(input("Enter second number: "))

print(f"{num_a} + {num_b}  = {num_a + num_b}")
print(f"{num_a} - {num_b}  = {num_a - num_b}")
print(f"{num_a} * {num_b}  = {num_a * num_b}")
print(f"{num_a} / {num_b}  = {num_a / num_b:.4f}")
print(f"{num_a} // {num_b} = {num_a // num_b}")
print(f"{num_a} % {num_b}  = {num_a % num_b}")
print(f"{num_a} ** {num_b} = {num_a ** num_b:.4f}")
```

Expected Output

```
Enter first number: 10
Enter second number: 3
10.0 + 3.0  = 13.0
10.0 - 3.0  = 7.0
10.0 * 3.0  = 30.0
10.0 / 3.0  = 3.3333
10.0 // 3.0 = 3.0
10.0 % 3.0  = 1.0
10.0 ** 3.0 = 1000.0000
```

Example 5 -- Complete BMI Calculator

This example brings together all concepts from Chapters 1 through 3: a descriptive header, multiple typed inputs, arithmetic across several variables, and formatted output.

```python
# --------------------------------------------------
# Module  : bmi_calculator.py
# Purpose : Collects user height and weight, computes BMI.
# Author  : Ayman Alzaid
# --------------------------------------------------

height_cm = float(input("Enter your height in centimetres (e.g. 175): "))
weight_kg = float(input("Enter your weight in kilograms (e.g. 70): "))

height_m  = height_cm / 100        # convert to metres
bmi       = weight_kg / (height_m ** 2)  # BMI formula

print(f"Height: {height_cm:.1f} cm  ({height_m:.2f} m)")
print(f"Weight: {weight_kg:.1f} kg")
print(f"Your BMI: {bmi:.2f}")
```

Expected Output

```
Enter your height in centimetres (e.g. 175): 175
Enter your weight in kilograms (e.g. 70): 70
```

```
Height: 175.0 cm  (1.75 m)
Weight: 70.0 kg
Your BMI: 22.86
```

The Active Learning Framework

The three pillars below apply this chapter's core concepts. Pillar 1 traces a multi-step input program with given values. Pillar 2 targets f-string edge cases, operator precedence surprises, and crash-point prediction. Pillar 3 audits a broken area calculator. Work through all three in sequence.

Active Learning Pillars: **P1** Trace the interpreter line by line. **P2** Predict the output before running. **P3** Audit and refactor to PEP 8 standards. Verify every prediction at the terminal.

Pillar 1 -- Logic Exercise: Tracing an Input Program

Tracing an interactive program requires substituting given user values into the trace exactly as the interpreter would receive them. Treat each given value as what the user typed at the keyboard.

Assume the user enters: First number: 15 Second number: 4

PILLAR 1 Logic Exercise

Instructions: Using the assumed input values above, trace the script one line at a time. Complete the Execution Trace Table. Record the exact value and type of every variable. Do not run the code.

Python

```python
# Pillar 1: Input Trace -- assume num_a = 15, num_b = 4

num_a = int(input("Enter first number: "))
num_b = int(input("Enter second number: "))
result_add = num_a + num_b
result_div = num_a / num_b
result_mod = num_a % num_b
print(f"Sum:      {result_add}")
print(f"Division: {result_div:.2f}")
```

```
print(f"Modulo:   {result_mod}")
```

Statement	num_a	num_b	Result Variable	Console Output
int(input(...)) first call	15 (int)	--	--	--
int(input(...)) second call	15	4 (int)	--	--
result_add = num_a + num_b	15	4	? compute	--
result_div = num_a / num_b	15	4	? compute	--
result_mod = num_a % num_b	15	4	? compute	--
print(f"Sum: ...")	15	4	19	? fill in
print(f"Division: ...")	15	4	3.75	? fill in
print(f"Modulo: ...")	15	4	3	? fill in

Challenge Questions: What type is result_div even though both inputs are int? What does result_mod tell you about how 15 divides by 4?

Pillar 2 -- Mysterious Output Puzzles

Four puzzles follow. Each tests a specific behavior: operator precedence inside f-strings, the crash point of a missing cast, round() behavior, and the variable assignment puzzle. Record predictions before running anything.

PILLAR 2 Mysterious Output Puzzles

Instructions: Predict every line of output for each puzzle before running anything. Record predictions first, then execute and compare.

Puzzle 3.1 -- Operator Precedence in f-Strings

Assume `a = 3` and `b = 4`. Predict all four outputs.

```python
# Puzzle 3.1: Precedence Inside f-Strings

a = 3
b = 4
```

```
print(f"A: {a + b * 2}")
print(f"B: {(a + b) * 2}")
print(f"C: {a ** b}")
print(f"D: {a ** b:.2f}")
```

Questions: Why do A and B differ? Does the :.2f specifier change the actual value or only how it displays?

Puzzle 3.2 -- The Missing Cast

Assume the user enters 8. Identify the exact crash line and error type.

```
# Puzzle 3.2: Missing Cast -- Assume user enters: 8

raw_input = input("Enter a number: ")  # no cast applied
doubled   = raw_input * 2
result    = doubled + 10
print(f"Result: {result}")
```

Questions: Which line crashes and with what error type? What does doubled actually contain before the crash?

Puzzle 3.3 -- The round() Surprise

Python 3 uses round-half-to-even (banker's rounding): when a value is exactly halfway, it rounds to the nearest even number. The last case in the code below has an additional twist from float representation. Predict each output.

```
# Puzzle 3.3: round() Behavior

print(round(2.5))    # .5 with even number to the left
print(round(3.5))    # .5 with odd number to the left
print(round(2.675, 2)) # floating-point precision trap
print(f"{2.675:.2f}")        # f-string version
```

Questions: Do round(2.5) and round(3.5) produce the same result? What does round(2.675, 2) return?

Puzzle 3.4 -- Assignment Is Not a Function Call

Assume the user enters "Alex" when prompted.

```python
# Puzzle 3.4: How many times does the program pause?

first_name = input("Enter your first name: ")
last_name  = first_name

print(f"Full name: {first_name} {last_name}")
print(f"Same? {first_name == last_name}")
```

Questions: How many times does the program pause for input? What does last_name hold and why? What does the second print display?

Pillar 3 -- Code Audit: Input Handling and Output Quality

The script below crashes at the arithmetic line. Beyond the missing cast, it also violates four PEP 8 conventions and uses string concatenation instead of f-strings. Identify every problem, record each in the audit table, then rewrite to production standards.

PILLAR 3 Code Audit -- Input Handling

Instructions: Identify every violation. Record each in the table. Then rewrite the entire script to production standards.

Non-Compliant Script

```python
l=input("length:")
w=input("width:")
A=l*w
print("area is: "+A)
```

#	Violation Found	Rule Broken	Corrected Pattern
1	l=input(...) no spaces around =	E225: Missing whitespace around operator	length = input(...)
2	Variables l, w, A: single letters and uppercase	Naming: use descriptive lowercase_snake_case	length, width, area
3	Prompt "length:" has no trailing space or format hint	UX: prompts must guide the user on expected format	input("Enter length in metres (e.g. 5.2): ")
4	No cast applied -- l and w are strings, l*w crashes	Type safety: always cast numeric input immediately	float(input(...))
5	"area is: " + A uses concatenation; A would need str()	Style: use f-strings for combining text and variables	f"Area: {area:.2f} square metres"

Production-Quality Refactored Script

```python
# --------------------------------------------------
# Module  : area_calculator.py
# Purpose : Collects rectangle dimensions, computes area.
# Author  : Ayman Alzaid
# --------------------------------------------------

length = float(input("Enter length in metres (e.g. 5.2): "))
width  = float(input("Enter width in metres (e.g. 3.0): "))

area   = length * width

print(f"Length: {length:.2f} m")
print(f"Width:  {width:.2f} m")
print(f"Area:   {area:.2f} square metres")
```

Coding Challenge: Personal Finance Calculator

Chapter 3 Coding Challenge
Objective: Build a personal finance calculator that collects user data, performs multi-step calculations, and displays formatted output. Every requirement below must appear in the solution.
>> Open with a PEP 8 compliant header comment block.
>> Collect three inputs with descriptive prompts: monthly salary (float), monthly rent (float), number of dependants (int).
>> Compute annual salary, total annual rent, and remaining annual income after rent.
>> Calculate the percentage of annual salary spent on rent. Display formatted to 1 decimal place.
>> Divide remaining income equally across all dependants. Display each share to 2 decimal places.
>> Use f-strings for every print() statement.

Chapter Summary

Concept	Key Takeaway
input()	Pauses execution and returns the user entry. Return type is always str.
The Cast Requirement	Any numeric input must be wrapped in int() or float() before arithmetic. Omitting it crashes the program.
Descriptive Prompts	Prompts must specify the expected format. A trailing space separates the prompt from the cursor.
f-Strings	Prefix with f and place expressions in {} to insert evaluated results inline.
:.2f Specifier	Formats a float to exactly N decimal places inside an f-string expression.
round(value, n)	Returns value rounded to n decimal places using banker's rounding in Python 3.
All Seven Operators	+ - * / // % ** all work on numeric input once the cast is applied.
ValueError	Raised when casting receives non-numeric text such as int("hello").
TypeError	Raised when incompatible types meet an operator, such as string + integer.

CHAPTER 4

Boolean Logic and Comparison Operators

Learning Objectives

1. Explain what a Boolean value is and describe the two states it can hold.
2. Evaluate expressions using all six comparison operators and predict whether each returns True or False.
3. Distinguish between the assignment operator = and the equality operator == and explain the consequences of confusing them.
4. Build compound Boolean expressions using the logical operators and, or, and not.
5. Apply truth table logic to predict the result of any combination of True and False operands.
6. Explain short-circuit evaluation and predict which side of a compound expression Python skips.
7. Apply Python's logical operator precedence (not >> and >> or) to evaluate complex expressions without parentheses.
8. Identify always-true and always-false logic errors and reconstruct the expression with the correct operator.

Theoretical Foundation

From Sequential to Decision-Based Execution

Every program written in the previous three chapters ran identically every time: line one, line two, line three, in order. That model works for calculations. It fails completely for any program that must respond differently to different conditions. A payroll system that gives every employee the same tax bracket is wrong. A login system that accepts every password is worse than useless. These programs need to decide.

The mechanism that makes decisions possible is the **Boolean value**. Every condition a program evaluates reduces to one of exactly two states: **True** or **False**. There is no third option. The entire structure of conditional logic is built on that binary foundation.

Boolean Values: True and False

Python's **bool** data type holds exactly two values: `True` and `False`. These are not strings. They are dedicated Boolean literals, always capitalized in Python. Lowercase `true` and `false` are undefined variable names that raise a NameError immediately.

Critical Rule: Boolean Literals Are Capitalized
Correct: `True` and `False` -- Python's built-in Boolean literals.
Wrong: `true` and `false` -- these raise a NameError.
Store in a variable: `is_ready = True` then use `is_ready` wherever a condition is needed.

Comparison Operators: Building Conditions

Comparison operators test the relationship between two values and return a Boolean. Python provides six. Each one asks a specific question and answers with True or False.

Operator	Meaning	Expression	Result	Common Mistake
==	Equal to	10 == 10	True	Using = instead of == assigns, not compares.
!=	Not equal to	10 != 5	True	Reads: "10 is not 5" -- True because they differ.
>	Greater than	7 > 12	False	Does not include equality. 7 > 7 is False.
<	Less than	3 < 8	True	Does not include equality. 8 < 8 is False.
>=	Greater or equal to	7 >= 7	True	Includes the boundary. 7 >= 7 is True.
<=	Less or equal to	9 <= 4	False	Includes the boundary. 4 <= 4 is True.

The = vs == Trap

The single equals sign (`=`) is the assignment operator. It stores a value. The double equals sign (`==`) is the equality comparison. It asks a question and returns True or False. Using `=` where `==` is intended does not always error immediately -- it silently produces wrong behavior. The rule is absolute: inside a condition, use `==`.

Assignment vs. Equality
Assignment (=): `score = 100` -- stores 100. Returns nothing. Not a question.
Equality (==): `score == 100` -- asks "is score 100?" Returns True or False.
Inside conditions: Always use ==. Writing `if score = 100:` is a SyntaxError in Python.

Logical Operators: and, or, not

The **and** operator requires both conditions to be True. The **or** operator requires only one. The **not** operator inverts a single Boolean value. These three operators combine comparison results into compound Boolean expressions.

Truth Tables: The Complete Logical Reference

A	B	A and B
True	True	True
True	False	False
False	True	False
False	False	False

A	B	A or B
True	True	True
True	False	True
False	True	True
False	False	False

A	not A
True	False
False	True

Short-Circuit Evaluation

Python does not always evaluate both sides of a compound expression. When the outcome is guaranteed from the left side, Python stops. For `and`: if the left is False, the whole expression is False -- right side skipped. For `or`: if the left is True, the whole expression is True -- right side skipped. This is **short-circuit evaluation**, and it has a direct safety consequence.

Short-Circuit Safety Pattern
Dangerous: `result = 10 / value` -- crashes if value is 0.
Safe: `result = (value != 0) and (10 / value > 2)` -- left side is False when value=0. Right side never executes.

Logical Operator Precedence

When a compound expression contains multiple logical operators without parentheses, Python applies them in fixed priority order: **not** first, then **and**, then **or**. Use parentheses to override this default when a different grouping is needed.

Figure 4.1 -- Logical Operator Evaluation Order

Priority 1 (Highest)		Priority 2		Priority 3 (Lowest)
not *Flips True/False*	>>	**and** *Both must be True*	>>	**or** *Either must be True*
`not True >> False`		`True and False >> False`		`True or False >> True`

The expression `not A or B and C` evaluates as `(not A) or (B and C)`. Without parentheses, the grouping is frequently misread. Always add parentheses when clarity is at stake.

Always-True and Always-False Logic Errors

These are the most common logic bugs in conditional logic. The code runs without crashing, but produces wrong answers silently.

Error Type	Broken Expression	Why It Fails	Correct Version
Always-False with and	x < 1 and x > 100	No number can be simultaneously less than 1 AND greater than 100.	x < 1 or x > 100
Always-True with or	x >= 0 or x < 0	Every number is either non-negative or negative. Always True.	x >= 0 and x < 100 (add a real constraint)
Wrong boundary	age > 18 and age > 65	Intended to check adults also seniors. Wrong direction.	age >= 18 and age <= 65

Formal Syntax and Declaration

Boolean Variable Declaration

Boolean variables follow standard assignment syntax: `is_active = True`. By convention, Boolean variable names should read as yes-or-no statements -- `is_active`, `has_permission`, `can_proceed`.

```python
# Comparison Expression Syntax

user_age        = 21
is_adult        = user_age >= 18   # stores True
is_exactly_21   = user_age == 21   # stores True
is_senior       = user_age >= 65   # stores False

print(is_adult)          # Output: True
print(is_senior)         # Output: False
print(type(is_adult))     # Output: <class 'bool'>
```

Expected Output
True
False
<class 'bool'>

Implementation and Code Examples

Example 1 -- All Six Comparison Operators

```python
# Example 1: All Six Comparison Operators

temperature = 37
```

```
print(temperature == 37)   # Equal to:           True
print(temperature != 36)   # Not equal to:       True
print(temperature > 38)    # Greater than:       False
print(temperature < 40)    # Less than:          True
print(temperature >= 37)   # Greater or equal:   True
print(temperature <= 36)   # Less or equal:      False
```

Expected Output

```
True
True
False
True
True
False
```

Example 2 -- Compound Conditions and Access Control

Three conditions each evaluate independently. The logical operators combine their Boolean results into one final access decision. Trace each sub-expression before applying the operator.

```python
# Example 2: Access Control with Compound Conditions

user_age    = 20
has_ticket  = True
is_banned   = False

age_ok     = user_age >= 18              # True
can_enter  = age_ok and has_ticket        # True and True >> True
access_ok  = can_enter and not is_banned  # True and not False >> True

print(f"Age check: {age_ok}")
print(f"Can enter: {can_enter}")
print(f"Access granted: {access_ok}")
```

Expected Output

```
Age check: True
Can enter: True
Access granted: True
```

Example 3 -- Short-Circuit Safety Guard

Division by zero crashes immediately. The left side of the `and` expression guards the right side. When the guard is False, the division never executes.

```python
# Example 3: Short-Circuit Safety

# Case A: divisor is zero -- guard fires, division never runs
divisor   = 0
numerator = 100
safe_result = (divisor != 0) and (numerator / divisor > 5)
print(f"Safe result: {safe_result}")  # Output: False -- no crash

# Case B: divisor is valid -- both sides evaluate
divisor     = 10
safe_result = (divisor != 0) and (numerator / divisor > 5)
print(f"Safe result: {safe_result}")  # Output: True
```

Expected Output

```
Safe result: False
Safe result: True
```

Example 4 -- Operator Precedence Without Parentheses

Python reads `not alpha or beta and gamma` as `(not alpha) or (beta and gamma)`. Comments in the code below trace every step.

```python
# Example 4: Precedence -- not before and before or

alpha = True
beta  = False
gamma = True

result = not alpha or beta and gamma

# Step trace:
# not alpha          >> not True     >> False
# beta and gamma     >> False and True >> False
# False or False     >> False

print(result)  # Output: False
```

Expected Output

```
False
```

Example 5 -- The Always-False Bug and Its Fix

```python
# Example 5: Always-False Bug -- and vs or

id_flag = 150  # should be flagged: outside range 1-100

# BROKEN: no number can be < 1 AND > 100 simultaneously
is_invalid_broken = (id_flag < 1) and (id_flag > 100)
print(f"Broken: {is_invalid_broken}")  # Always False!

# FIXED: or is correct -- out of range on EITHER side
is_invalid_fixed  = (id_flag < 1) or (id_flag > 100)
print(f"Fixed:  {is_invalid_fixed}")   # True: 150 > 100
```

Expected Output
`Broken: False`
`Fixed:  True`

The Active Learning Framework

The three pillars below apply Boolean logic through targeted challenges. Pillar 1 traces a compound expression step by step. Pillar 2 presents four edge cases that expose the most common misreadings. Pillar 3 audits a broken watchdog script. Work through all three in sequence.

Active Learning Pillars: **P1** Trace the interpreter line by line. **P2** Predict the output before running. **P3** Audit and refactor to PEP 8 standards. Verify every prediction at the terminal.

Pillar 1 -- Logic Exercise: Expression Trace

Use these values throughout the trace: `speed = 85`, `fuel_level = 15`, `engine_ok = True`. Evaluate the expression below one step at a time applying precedence: comparisons first, then not, then and, then or.

PILLAR 1 Logic Exercise
Instructions: Fill in the Step-by-Step Trace Table using the given variable values. Do not run the code.

Python

```python
# Pillar 1: Expression Trace

speed      = 85
fuel_level = 15
engine_ok  = True

alert = (speed > 80) and (fuel_level < 20) or not engine_ok
print(alert)
```

Step	Sub-Expression	Substituted Values	Result
1	speed > 80	85 > 80	?
2	fuel_level < 20	15 < 20	?
3	not engine_ok	not True	?
4	(Step 1) and (Step 2)	? and ?	?
5	(Step 4) or (Step 3)	? or ?	? Final

Challenge Questions: What is the final value of alert? If speed were 75, how would the result change? Which side does short-circuit skip if Step 4 is True?

Pillar 2 -- Mysterious Output Puzzles

Four puzzles follow. The not binding trap, the always-false and, short-circuit side-effects, and chained comparisons. Predict every output before running anything.

PILLAR 2 Mysterious Output Puzzles

Instructions: Predict every output before running any code. Record predictions first, then execute and compare.

Puzzle 4.1 -- The not Binding Trap

The `not` operator binds only to the immediate value to its right. The difference between these two expressions is parentheses placement only.

```python
# Puzzle 4.1: not Binding

a = True
b = False

print(not a or b)    # not binds only to a
print(not (a or b))  # not applies to (a or b)
```

Questions: Do both produce the same output? Trace each with precedence rules. Why does parentheses placement change the result?

Puzzle 4.2 -- The Silent Always-False

Predict the output for all three test values. This check is meant to catch invalid scores outside 0-100.

```python
# Puzzle 4.2: Always-False Check

def check_score(score):
    is_invalid = score < 0 and score > 100
    print(f"Score {score} invalid: {is_invalid}")

check_score(-5)
check_score(50)
check_score(150)
```

Questions: Does any call return True as intended? Which operator must replace and to make the function work?

Puzzle 4.3 -- Short-Circuit Skipping

Predict how many times `counter_fn()` executes across all four calls.

```python
# Puzzle 4.3: Short-Circuit Side Effects

call_count = 0

def counter_fn():
    global call_count
    call_count += 1
    return True

False and counter_fn()  # Case A
True  and counter_fn()  # Case B
True  or  counter_fn()  # Case C
False or  counter_fn()  # Case D

print(f"counter_fn called {call_count} times")
```

Questions: How many total calls does counter_fn() receive? Which two cases short-circuit and skip it? What does the final print display?

Puzzle 4.4 -- Chained Comparisons

Python supports chained comparisons. `1 < x < 10` is shorthand for `x > 1 and x < 10`. Predict all four outputs.

```
Python

# Puzzle 4.4: Chained Comparisons

x = 5

print(1 < x < 10)
print(10 > x > 1)
print(1 < x <= 5)
print(5 < x < 10)
```

Questions: What are the four outputs? The third includes x <= 5 with x = 5 -- does that boundary pass? What does the fourth tell you?

Pillar 3 -- Code Audit: Logic Operator Errors

The script contains three logic errors: an always-false and expression, a redundant == False comparison, and missing parentheses that misgroup the intended condition. Identify each, record in the table, then rewrite the complete script.

PILLAR 3 Code Audit -- Logic Operator Errors

Instructions: Identify every logic error. Record each in the table. Rewrite the script so it correctly implements the described business rule.

Non-Compliant Script

```
Python

# Business rule: alert if (load > 90 AND admin absent) OR (load > 99)

server_load   = 95
admin_online  = False
```

```python
admin_absent  = admin_online == False  # BUG 1: redundant == False
overloaded    = server_load > 90 and server_load < 0  # BUG 2: always-False
alert         = overloaded and admin_absent or server_load > 99  # BUG 3: missing parens
print(f"Alert: {alert}")
```

#	Error Found	Rule Broken	Corrected Pattern
1	admin_online == False -- comparing bool to False	Never use == True or == False on a Boolean. Use directly or with not.	admin_absent = not admin_online
2	server_load > 90 and server_load < 0 -- impossible	No value can be > 90 and < 0 simultaneously. Always evaluates False.	Remove the < 0 condition; use correct threshold logic.
3	No parentheses -- and/or precedence groups expression incorrectly	Add parentheses when mixing and and or to make intent explicit.	alert = (server_load > 90 and admin_absent) or (server_load > 99)

Production-Quality Refactored Script

```python
# --------------------------------------------------
# Module  : server_watchdog.py
# Purpose : Triggers alert based on load and admin status.
# Author  : Ayman Alzaid
# --------------------------------------------------

server_load   = 95
admin_online  = False

admin_absent  = not admin_online  # cleaner than == False

alert         = (server_load > 90 and admin_absent) or (server_load > 99)

print(f"Load: {server_load}%  |  Alert: {alert}")  # Output: True
```

Coding Challenge: Event Access Validator

Chapter 4 Coding Challenge

Objective: Build an event access validation system using Boolean logic. Collect user data and evaluate a multi-condition access policy. No if statements -- compute and print only Boolean values.

>> Collect three inputs: user age (int), ticket type as "standard" or "vip" (str), and years of membership (int).

>> Compute five Boolean variables: is_adult, has_vip, is_member, is_senior_member (years >= 5), and is_minor.

>> Compute can_access: is_adult AND (has_vip OR is_senior_member).

>> Compute needs_escort: is_minor AND is_member.

>> Compute vip_lounge: has_vip AND is_adult AND is_senior_member.

>> Print all five variables with descriptive f-string labels.

>> Add a plain-English comment above each compound expression explaining what rule it checks.

Chapter Summary

Concept	Key Takeaway
Boolean Values	Two states only: True or False. Always capitalized. Return type of every comparison.
== vs =	= assigns a value. == tests equality. Never use = inside a condition.
Six Comparison Operators	==, !=, >, <, >=, <= each return True or False. >= and <= include the boundary.
and	Both sides must be True. If left is False, right side is skipped.
or	At least one side must be True. If left is True, right side is skipped.
not	Inverts a single Boolean. not True is False. not False is True.
Precedence Order	not first, then and, then or. Use parentheses to override.
Short-Circuit	Python stops evaluating when the outcome is guaranteed. Protects against runtime errors.
Always-False Bug	x < 0 and x > 100 is logically impossible. Use or for out-of-range checks.
Redundant == True/False	Never write is_active == True. Write is_active. Never write flag == False. Write not flag.

CHAPTER 5

Python Conditionals

Learning Objectives

1. Write correctly structured if, if-else, and if-elif-else statements with proper colon and indentation syntax.
2. Explain the role of the colon and four-space indentation in defining a conditional code block.
3. Apply the one-path-wins rule to predict which block executes in a multi-branch chain.
4. Trace the execution path of an if-elif-else chain given specific input values.
5. Write nested if statements and explain when nesting is appropriate versus when logical operators produce cleaner code.
6. Combine comparison and logical operators inside conditional expressions to test compound conditions.
7. Identify and correct common conditional errors: unreachable branches, missing colons, indentation faults, and redundant == True checks.
8. Build a complete interactive program that uses if-elif-else to produce different outputs based on user input.

Theoretical Foundation

From Boolean Expressions to Execution Paths

Chapter 4 established the logical foundation: Boolean expressions evaluate to **True** or **False**. That foundation answers a question but does nothing with the answer. Chapter 5 connects the answer to action. The **conditional statement** reads the Boolean result and routes execution down one of two or more distinct code paths. The program no longer runs every line. It evaluates a condition and runs *only* the lines belonging to the branch that matched.

This is the structural shift in program architecture. A sequential script is a single road. A conditional script is a network of roads with decision points. The condition at each decision point is always a Boolean expression. The interpreter reads it, gets True or False, and turns accordingly.

The if Statement: Opening a Conditional Block

The **if** statement is the core decision tool in Python. It evaluates a Boolean expression. If the expression is True, the indented block directly beneath it executes. If the expression is False, the entire block is skipped and execution jumps to the next unindented line. Nothing inside the block runs. Python does not execute it partially.

Two structural rules govern every `if` statement and every conditional construct in Python. **Rule 1:** The condition line must end with a colon (`:`). The colon signals that an indented block follows. Omit it and Python raises a **SyntaxError** immediately. **Rule 2:** Every line inside the block must be indented by exactly **four spaces**. Python uses indentation to define block membership. A line at the left margin is outside the block. A line indented by four spaces is inside it.

The Two Non-Negotiable Syntax Rules
Rule 1 — The Colon: Every `if`, `elif`, and `else` line must end with `:`. This is not optional punctuation. It is a hard syntax requirement.
Rule 2 — Four-Space Indentation: Every statement inside a conditional block must be indented by exactly 4 spaces. Mixing tabs and spaces, or using 2 or 3 spaces, raises an `IndentationError`.

The else Statement: The Fallback Path

The **else** statement provides a fallback path. It carries no condition of its own. It runs if and only if every condition above it evaluated to False. An `else` block is optional. Many `if` statements do not need one. But when a program must guarantee that exactly one path always executes regardless of input, `else` provides that guarantee.

An `else` block can never appear before an `if` block. It cannot carry a condition. Writing `else score > 50:` is a **SyntaxError**. The condition belongs on the `if` or `elif` line. `else` receives whatever condition was not caught by any earlier branch.

The elif Statement: Multi-Branch Routing

When a program needs to choose among more than two outcomes, **elif** (short for "else if") chains additional conditions onto the structure. Python reads the chain from top to bottom. It evaluates each condition in sequence. The first condition that evaluates to True wins. Its block executes. All remaining `elif` and `else` blocks are skipped entirely. This behavior is called the **one-path-wins rule**.

The one-path-wins rule has a direct consequence: once a condition fires, subsequent conditions are never evaluated. This creates the possibility of an **unreachable branch** — a condition that can never fire because an earlier, broader condition already catches every case that would have matched it. Unreachable branches do not produce errors. The program runs normally but the branch silently never executes. Finding and removing them is a standard code audit task.

Nested Conditionals

A **nested conditional** is an `if` statement placed inside the block of another `if` statement. The inner `if` only runs when the outer condition is True. Nesting is necessary when a second decision depends entirely on the first. It is unnecessary when two conditions could be combined into a single compound expression using `and` or `or`.

Nesting vs. Logical Operators: Which to Choose

Use nesting when: the inner decision is only meaningful if the outer condition passed. Example: check if a file exists before checking its size.

Use and/or when: both conditions test the same input and could be written as one expression. Example: `if age >= 18 and has_ticket:` is cleaner than nesting two separate if statements.

Danger zone: deeply nested conditions (3 or more levels) are a strong signal the logic needs restructuring.

Common Conditional Errors

Error Type	What It Looks Like	What Goes Wrong	How to Fix It
Missing colon	if score > 90	SyntaxError: expected ":"	if score > 90:
Wrong indentation	if x > 0: print("yes")	IndentationError: expected indented block	Indent the print statement 4 spaces
Using = instead of ==	if score = 100:	SyntaxError in Python (unlike some languages)	if score == 100:
Redundant == True	if is_ready == True:	Works but is unnecessary and unidiomatic	if is_ready:
Unreachable elif	if x > 0: ... elif x > 10: ...	The elif never fires -- x > 0 catches all positives	Swap the order: check x > 10 first
No else fallback	if/elif chain with no else	Nothing executes when all conditions are False	Add an else block for the default case

Formal Syntax and Declaration

if Statement Syntax

The minimal conditional structure is a single `if` statement. The condition is any expression that evaluates to True or False. The block contains one or more indented statements.

```python
# if Statement -- Formal Syntax

if condition:
    # indented block executes when condition is True
    statement_one
```

```
    statement_two

# this line is outside the block -- always executes
next_statement
```

if-else Syntax

Adding `else` provides a guaranteed fallback path. Exactly one of the two blocks always executes. `else` carries no condition and no colon-expression, only a colon.

```python
# if-else -- Formal Syntax

if condition:
    # block runs when condition is True
    true_block_statement
else:
    # block runs when condition is False
    false_block_statement
```

if-elif-else Syntax

The full multi-branch structure. Python evaluates conditions from top to bottom. The first True condition wins. All others are skipped. `else` is optional but provides the guaranteed fallback.

```python
# if-elif-else -- Formal Syntax (one-path-wins)

if condition_one:
    block_one  # runs if condition_one is True
elif condition_two:
    block_two  # runs if condition_one False AND condition_two True
elif condition_three:
    block_three  # runs if both above False AND this True
else:
    fallback_block  # runs only if ALL conditions above were False
```

Element	Carries a Condition?	Runs When...	Required?
if	Yes	Its condition is True	Yes — must open the structure
elif	Yes	All prior conditions were False AND its condition is True	No — zero or many allowed
else	No	All prior conditions were False	No — at most one, always last

Implementation and Code Examples

Example 1 -- Simple if Statement

The simplest conditional: one condition, one block. If the condition is False, the indented block is skipped and execution continues at the next unindented line. Notice the blank line after the block -- this is PEP 8 convention for readability.

Python

```
# Example 1: Simple if Statement

temperature = 38

if temperature > 37:  # evaluates to True
    print("Warning: elevated temperature detected.")
    print("Please consult a physician.")

# This line is outside the block -- always runs
print("Temperature check complete.")
```

Expected Output

```
Warning: elevated temperature detected.
Please consult a physician.
Temperature check complete.
```

Example 2 -- if-else: Two Guaranteed Paths

Adding `else` guarantees that exactly one path always runs. The program cannot fall through to the next section without executing some block. Study the output for both values of `age` in the comment below the example.

```python
# Example 2: if-else Structure

age = 16

if age >= 18:
    print("Access granted. Welcome.")
else:
    print("Access denied. You must be 18 or older.")

# With age = 16: condition 16 >= 18 is False >> else fires
# With age = 20: condition 20 >= 18 is True  >> if fires
```

Expected Output

```
Access denied. You must be 18 or older.
```

Example 3 -- if-elif-else: Grade Classification

This example demonstrates the one-path-wins rule across five branches. Python reads from the top. The first condition that is True fires its block, and the entire remaining structure is skipped. Trace through with score = 85 and verify which branch catches it.

```python
# Example 3: Multi-Branch Grade Classification

score = 85

if score >= 90:
    grade = "A  -- Exceptional"
elif score >= 80:
    grade = "B  -- Strong"      # score = 85 >> this fires
```

```
elif score >= 70:
    grade = "C  -- Satisfactory"
elif score >= 60:
    grade = "D  -- Needs Improvement"
else:
    grade = "F  -- Failing"

print(f"Score: {score}  |  Grade: {grade}")
```

Expected Output

```
Score: 85  |  Grade: B  -- Strong
```

Example 4 -- Compound Conditions Inside if Statements

The Boolean logic operators from Chapter 4 work directly inside `if` conditions. This eliminates unnecessary nesting when multiple conditions test the same subject. Study the contrast between the nested version and the flat compound version below.

```
Python
# Example 4: Compound Conditions vs Nested ifs

user_age    = 25
has_account = True
is_verified = True

# NESTED VERSION -- works but adds unnecessary depth
if user_age >= 18:
    if has_account:
        if is_verified:
            print("Access granted (nested).")

# FLAT VERSION -- cleaner, identical behavior
if user_age >= 18 and has_account and is_verified:
    print("Access granted (flat).")
```

Expected Output

```
Access granted (nested).
Access granted (flat).
```

Example 5 -- Complete Interactive Program: ATM Dispatcher

This example brings together input collection from Chapter 3, type casting, and a complete `if-elif-else` decision structure. Read the three business rules in the header comment before tracing the logic.

```python
# --------------------------------------------------
# Module  : atm_dispatcher.py
# Purpose : Processes a withdrawal request against rules.
# Rules   : 1. Amount <= 0 is invalid.
#           2. Amount > balance is insufficient funds.
#           3. Otherwise: approve and deduct.
# Author  : Ayman Alzaid
# --------------------------------------------------

balance    = float(input("Enter your account balance: $"))
withdrawal = float(input("Enter withdrawal amount:   $"))

if withdrawal <= 0:
    print("Error: withdrawal amount must be greater than zero.")
elif withdrawal > balance:
    print("Declined: insufficient funds.")
    print(f"Available balance: ${balance:.2f}")
else:
    balance -= withdrawal
    print(f"Dispensing: ${withdrawal:.2f}")
    print(f"Remaining balance: ${balance:.2f}")
```

Expected Output

```
Enter your account balance: $500.00
Enter withdrawal amount:   $120.00
Dispensing: $120.00
Remaining balance: $380.00
```

The Active Learning Framework

The three pillars below apply conditional logic with three direct challenges. Pillar 1 requires tracing a complete `if-elif-else` chain to determine the exact execution path. Pillar 2 presents four puzzles on the one-path-wins rule, unreachable branches, independent `if` vs `elif`, and nested conditionals. Pillar 3 audits a common beginner conditional script with four violations.

Active Learning Pillars: **P1** Trace the interpreter line by line. **P2** Predict the output before running. **P3** Audit and refactor to PEP 8 standards. Verify every prediction at the terminal.

Pillar 1 -- Logic Exercise: Execution Path Trace

Tracing a conditional chain means reading each condition in order and deciding whether it is True or False given the current variable values. The moment a True condition is found, its block executes and all remaining branches are skipped. Apply the one-path-wins rule strictly: no matter how many conditions are True in theory, only the first one fires.

Trace Rule 1: Evaluate each condition from top to bottom using the given values. **Trace Rule 2:** The first True condition fires its block and the chain ends. **Trace Rule 3:** If no condition is True, the `else` block fires.

PILLAR 1 Logic Exercise

Instructions: Using the variable values given in the script, trace the execution path one condition at a time. Complete the Execution Path Table. Record True or False for each condition and identify exactly which block executes. Do not run the code.

Python

```python
# Pillar 1: Execution Path Trace

speed      = 75
is_raining = True

if speed > 100:
    print("Alert: dangerously high speed.")
elif speed > 80 and is_raining:
    print("Warning: high speed in wet conditions.")
elif speed > 60 and is_raining:
    print("Caution: moderate speed, rainy conditions.")
elif speed > 60:
```

```
    print("Advisory: reduce speed for safety.")
else:
    print("All clear: safe speed.")
```

Execution Path Table

Condition Evaluated	Substituted Expression	Result	Action
speed > 100	75 > 100	? fill in	? fires / skips
speed > 80 and is_raining	75 > 80 and True	? fill in	? fires / skips
speed > 60 and is_raining	75 > 60 and True	? fill in	? fires / skips
speed > 60	75 > 60	not reached	not reached
else	no condition	not reached	not reached

Challenge Questions: Which block executes? Even though speed > 60 and speed > 80 are both potentially relevant, why does the third elif fire instead of the fourth? What would change if is_raining were False?

Pillar 2 -- Mysterious Output Puzzles: Predict Before You Run

Four puzzles follow. Each targets a specific behavior of conditional structures: the priority routing trap, the unreachable branch, the difference between chained `if` statements versus `elif`, and the nested else ambiguity. Predict the exact console output for each puzzle before running anything.

PILLAR 2 Mysterious Output Puzzles

Instructions: Predict the complete console output for each puzzle. Write every prediction down before running any code. Then execute and compare against the actual results.

Puzzle 5.1 -- The Priority Routing Trap

The one-path-wins rule has a direct consequence when conditions overlap. A broader condition placed above a narrower one will catch cases the narrower one was meant to handle. Predict exactly what this script prints, then explain which block fires and why the others never execute.

```python
# Puzzle 5.1: Priority Routing Trap

current_speed = 75
```

```python
if current_speed > 50:
    print("Speed Alert: Moderate pace")
elif current_speed > 70:
    print("Speed Alert: Fast pace")
else:
    print("Speed Alert: Normal pace")
```

Questions: What single line does the script print? Speed 75 is both > 50 and > 70 -- so why does only one branch fire? What order change would make the "Fast pace" branch reachable?

Puzzle 5.2 -- The Independent ifs vs elif Chain

Two separate `if` statements are not an `elif` chain. Each `if` starts a fresh evaluation. Predict how many lines print for both scripts and explain the structural difference.

```python
# Puzzle 5.2: Two separate ifs vs elif chain

account_balance = 120

# Script A: two INDEPENDENT if statements
if account_balance > 100:
    account_balance -= 20
if account_balance > 50:
    account_balance -= 30
print(account_balance)

# Script B: elif chain -- only the first True fires
account_balance = 120  # reset
if account_balance > 100:
    account_balance -= 20
elif account_balance > 50:
    account_balance -= 30
print(account_balance)
```

Questions: What does Script A print? What does Script B print? Why are the results different even though the conditions look similar? How many deductions occur in each script?

Puzzle 5.3 -- The Unreachable Branch

An unreachable branch is a condition that can never fire because an earlier condition catches every case it would match. Identify which branch is unreachable, explain why, and predict the output for all three test calls.

```
• • •  Python

# Puzzle 5.3: Unreachable Branch

def classify(score):
    if score >= 50:
        print("Pass")
    elif score >= 80:
        print("Merit")
    elif score >= 95:
        print("Distinction")
    else:
        print("Fail")

classify(30)
classify(70)
classify(97)
```

Questions: What are the three outputs? Which branch is unreachable and why can it never fire? What is the correct order for the conditions to make all four branches reachable?

Puzzle 5.4 -- The Nested else Surprise

When `if` statements are nested, each `else` belongs to its nearest `if` -- not the outer one. Predict both outputs and explain which if each else is paired with.

```
• • •  Python

# Puzzle 5.4: Nested else -- which if does it belong to?

x = 10
y = 3

if x > 5:
    if y > 5:
        print("Both large")
    else:
        print("x large, y small")
```

```
else:
    print("x is not large")

# Now test with x = 3, y = 10
x = 3
y = 10

if x > 5:
    if y > 5:
        print("Both large")
    else:
        print("x large, y small")
else:
    print("x is not large")
```

Questions: What does the first block print with x=10, y=3? What does the second block print with x=3, y=10? In the first run, which if does the inner else belong to? Why does "x is not large" never print in the first run?

Pillar 3 -- Code Audit: Conditional Structure Violations

The script below attempts to validate a user's login attempt. It contains five violations: a missing colon, a redundant `== True` comparison, an unreachable `elif` branch, a deeply nested structure that should be flattened, and a non-descriptive variable name. Identify every violation, record each in the audit table, then rewrite the complete script to production standards.

PILLAR 3 Code Audit -- Conditional Structure

Instructions: Identify every violation in the non-compliant script. Record each in the audit table with the specific rule it breaks. Then rewrite the complete script to production standards.

Non-Compliant Script

```python
# login checker

u = input("username:")
p = input("password:")
```

```
valid_user = (u == "admin")
valid_pass = (p == "secret")

if valid_user == True      # BUG 1: redundant == True
    if valid_pass == True:
        print("Welcome, admin!")
    elif valid_user:  # BUG 3: unreachable
        print("User valid but something failed.")
    else:
        print("Wrong password.")
else:
    print("Unknown user.")
```

Violation Audit Table

#	Violation Found	Rule Broken	Corrected Pattern
1	valid_user == True -- redundant Boolean comparison	Never compare a bool to True using ==. Use the variable directly.	if valid_user:
2	if valid_user == True missing the colon (:)	Syntax rule: every if line must end with a colon.	if valid_user:
3	elif valid_user: is unreachable -- we are already inside if valid_user block	Logic rule: inside if valid_user:, valid_user is always True. The elif can never fire.	Remove it. The else handles the wrong-password case.
4	Deeply nested if inside if -- can be flattened	Clarity rule: use and to combine conditions when both test the same subject.	if valid_user and valid_pass:
5	Variables u and p are non-descriptive single letters	Naming rule: variables must describe their content.	username, password

Production-Quality Refactored Script

```python
# -----------------------------------------------------
# Module   : login_checker.py
# Purpose  : Validates username and password against
#            stored credentials and reports the result.
# Author   : Ayman Alzaid
# -----------------------------------------------------

username = input("Enter username: ")
```

```
password = input("Enter password: ")

# Flat compound condition -- no unnecessary nesting
if username == "admin" and password == "secret":
    print("Access granted. Welcome, admin!")
elif username == "admin":
    print("Incorrect password. Access denied.")
else:
    print("Unknown username. Access denied.")
```

Coding Challenge: Ticket Price Calculator

Chapter 5 Coding Challenge

Objective: Build a complete ticket pricing engine that collects user details and applies a multi-tier pricing policy using an if-elif-else chain. Every requirement below must be satisfied.

>> Open with a PEP 8 compliant header comment block: module name, author, date, and description.

>> Collect three inputs: customer age (int), membership status as "yes" or "no" (str), and day of visit as "weekday" or "weekend" (str).

>> Apply this pricing policy using an if-elif-else chain: age < 5 is free, age < 12 is child price ($8.00), age >= 65 is senior price ($10.00), member is "yes" is member price ($12.00), weekend day is $18.00, else standard price is $15.00.

>> Store the final ticket price in a variable and apply a 10% weekend surcharge if day is "weekend" and the customer is not already free.

>> Print a formatted receipt using f-strings showing all inputs and the final price to 2 decimal places.

>> Add a plain-English comment above each condition in the chain explaining the business rule it enforces.

Chapter Summary

Concept	Key Takeaway
if statement	Evaluates a Boolean condition. Runs the indented block if True, skips it if False.
else statement	Fallback path. Runs when all prior conditions in the chain were False. Carries no condition.
elif statement	Additional condition in a chain. Evaluated only if all prior conditions were False.
One-Path-Wins Rule	In an if-elif-else chain, exactly one block executes. The first True condition wins. All others are skipped.
Colon (:)	Required at the end of every if, elif, and else line. Omitting it raises a SyntaxError.
Four-Space Indentation	Every statement inside a conditional block must be indented by exactly 4 spaces.
Unreachable Branch	An elif condition that can never fire because an earlier, broader condition already catches all matching cases.
Nested Conditionals	An if statement inside another if block. Use when the inner decision depends entirely on the outer one.
Flat vs. Nested	Combine conditions with and/or when both test the same subject. Avoid nesting what can be flattened.
Redundant == True	Never write if is_ready == True. Write if is_ready. Never write == False. Write not flag.

CHAPTER 6

The Python match-case Statement

Python Version Requirement

This chapter requires Python 3.10 or later. The match-case statement was introduced in Python 3.10 (released October 2021) and does not exist in earlier versions. On Python 3.9 or below, every code example in this chapter will raise a SyntaxError with no explanation.

Verify your version before proceeding: `python --version` or `python3 --version` The output must show 3.10.x or higher.

To upgrade: Download the latest Python release from python.org/downloads. University lab systems can be checked with your IT department.

Learning Objectives

1. Explain what structural pattern matching is and identify the situations where match-case produces cleaner code than if-elif-else.
2. Write a correctly structured match statement with multiple case clauses and a wildcard fallback using case _:.
3. Explain why match-case does not fall through to subsequent cases after a match is found.
4. Use the | operator inside a case clause to match multiple values in a single branch.
5. Apply guard conditions (case x if condition:) to add a Boolean filter to a pattern.
6. Trace the execution path of a match statement given a specific input value.
7. Identify the appropriate use case for match-case versus if-elif-else and choose the right tool for a given problem.

Theoretical Foundation

The Problem match-case Solves

Chapter 5 introduced `if-elif-else` chains for multi-branch decision making. That structure is the correct tool when each branch tests a different kind of condition: one branch checks an age range, another checks a string value, another checks a Boolean. But when a program needs to route behavior based on *one variable's specific values* -- a menu selection, a command code, a status label -- the `elif` chain becomes repetitive. Every branch repeats the same variable name and the same `==` operator.

Python 3.10 introduced the **match-case statement** to handle exactly this pattern. Instead of cascading through conditions sequentially, `match` takes one value, evaluates it once at the top, and drops it into the correct `case` branch directly. The code reads like a routing table rather than a chain of questions.

Version Requirement

Python 3.10 or later is required. The match-case statement does not exist in Python 3.9 or earlier. Verify your version by running `python --version` in your terminal before executing examples in this chapter. If your version is below 3.10, the interpreter will raise a SyntaxError.

How match-case Works: One Entry, One Exit

A `match` statement reads its subject value once at the top. It then compares the result against each `case` pattern from top to bottom. The first case whose pattern matches the subject value executes its block. All remaining cases are skipped entirely. This is identical to the one-path-wins rule from Chapter 5, but the selection mechanism is pattern matching rather than Boolean condition evaluation.

There is no **fall-through** in Python's `match`. In some languages (notably C and JavaScript), a matched case continues executing into the next case unless explicitly stopped. Python does not do this. The first matching case runs its block and the `match` statement ends. No additional cases are evaluated.

The Wildcard Case: case _

The underscore (_) is Python's wildcard pattern. It matches anything and everything. A `case _`: block at the end of a `match` statement serves the same role as `else` in an `if-elif-else` chain: it catches every value that did not match any earlier case. It is optional, but without it, a value that matches no case simply produces no output and no error. For user-facing programs, always include a wildcard to handle unexpected input.

When to Use match-case vs if-elif-else

These two tools are not interchangeable in all situations. The practical rule: when every branch tests the same variable against a specific value, match-case is the cleaner choice. When branches test different variables, calculated ranges, or conditions built from multiple inputs, if-elif is the right tool.

Situation	Best Tool	Reason
Testing one variable against many specific values	match-case	Cleaner syntax, no variable repetition, reads like a routing table.
Testing different variables in each branch	if-elif-else	match only tests one subject. Different variables need separate conditions.

Situation	Best Tool	Reason
Testing ranges or inequalities (age > 18)	if-elif-else	match-case matches exact values or patterns, not ranges by default.
Menu selection, command dispatch, status routing	match-case	Exactly the use case match-case was designed for.
Complex compound conditions with and/or	if-elif-else	Guard conditions in match-case can help but if-elif is clearer for complex logic.

Figure 6.1 -- match-case vs if-elif-else Execution Model

The diagram below compares how each structure routes execution. The key difference: `if-elif` evaluates conditions sequentially and may test different subjects at each step. `match` evaluates its subject once and matches the result against fixed patterns.

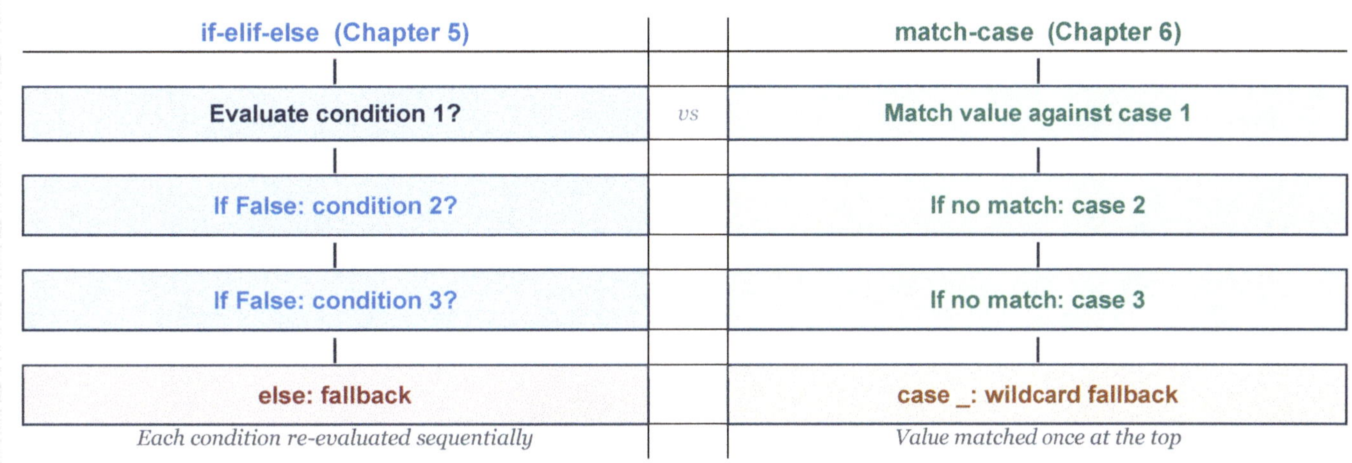

The | Operator: Matching Multiple Values

A single `case` clause can match more than one value using the | operator. Writing `case "red" | "orange" | "yellow":` creates a single branch that fires when the subject equals any of those three values. This eliminates the need to write separate identical branches for values that share the same behavior.

Guard Conditions: case x if condition

A **guard condition** is an if expression attached to a case clause. The syntax places `if` followed by any Boolean expression after the pattern. The case only fires if the pattern matches *and* the guard evaluates to True. This is how `match-case` handles range checks or computed conditions that go beyond simple value equality.

Formal Syntax and Declaration

Basic match-case Syntax

The `match` keyword is followed by the subject expression and a colon. Each `case` clause is indented one level, followed by its pattern and a colon. The case's code block is indented a second level -- four spaces inside the case, eight from the left margin.

```python
# match-case -- Formal Syntax

match subject_expression:
    case pattern_one:
        # block runs when subject matches pattern_one
        statement_one
    case pattern_two:
        # block runs when subject matches pattern_two
        statement_two
    case _:
        # wildcard: runs when no pattern above matched
        fallback_statement
```

Element	Syntax	Required?	Behaviour
match keyword	match subject:	Yes	Opens the structure. Subject is evaluated once.
case clause	case value:	Yes (at least one)	Matches subject against value. Fires if equal.
case with |	case "a" | "b":	No	Fires if subject equals any of the listed values.
case with guard	case x if x > 0:	No	Fires if pattern matches AND guard is True.
wildcard	case _:	No (recommended)	Matches everything. Acts as the else fallback.

Syntax Rules and Indentation

The same indentation discipline from Chapter 5 applies. The `match` line ends with a colon. Each `case` line is indented four spaces from `match` and also ends with a colon. The code inside each case is indented eight spaces from the left margin (four from `match`, four from `case`). Mixing these levels raises an `IndentationError`.

Implementation and Code Examples

Example 1 -- Basic match-case: Menu Router

The most direct use of `match-case`: one variable, multiple specific string values, one action per value. Compare the readability against an equivalent `if-elif-else` chain. The `match` version eliminates the repeated `command ==` on every branch.

Python

```python
# Example 1: match-case Menu Router

command = input("Enter command (start / stop / status / quit): ")

match command:
    case "start":
        print("System starting...")
    case "stop":
        print("System stopping...")
    case "status":
        print("System is running normally.")
    case "quit":
        print("Goodbye.")
    case _:
        print(f"Unknown command: {command}")
```

Expected Output

```
Enter command (start / stop / status / quit): status
System is running normally.
```

Example 2 -- Matching Integers: HTTP Status Router

`match-case` works equally well with integer values. This example routes HTTP status codes to human-readable messages. Without `match`, this would require a chain of `elif status_code == 200:`, `elif status_code == 404:`, and so on for every code.

```python
# Example 2: Matching Integer Values

status_code = int(input("Enter HTTP status code: "))

match status_code:
    case 200:
        print("200 OK -- Request succeeded.")
    case 301:
        print("301 Moved Permanently -- Resource relocated.")
    case 404:
        print("404 Not Found -- Resource does not exist.")
    case 500:
        print("500 Internal Server Error -- Server fault.")
    case _:
        print(f"{status_code} -- Unrecognised status code.")
```

Expected Output

```
Enter HTTP status code: 404
404 Not Found -- Resource does not exist.
```

Example 3 -- The | Operator: Grouping Values

When several values share identical behavior, the `|` operator combines them into one case clause. This example classifies user-entered day names into working days, weekend days, and invalid input. Without `|`, five separate identical case blocks would be required for the weekdays alone.

```python
# Example 3: | Operator -- Grouping Multiple Values

day = input("Enter day name: ").lower()
```

```python
match day:
    case "monday" | "tuesday" | "wednesday" | "thursday" | "friday":
        print(f"{day.capitalize()} is a working day.")
    case "saturday" | "sunday":
        print(f"{day.capitalize()} is a weekend day.")
    case _:
        print(f'"{day}" is not a valid day name.')
```

Expected Output
Enter day name: Wednesday
Wednesday is a working day.

Example 4 -- Guard Conditions: Adding Boolean Filters

A guard condition extends a case clause with an `if` expression. The case only fires when the pattern matches *and* the guard is True. This is how `match-case` handles numeric ranges, which case patterns alone cannot handle -- patterns match exact values only, not ranges. The captured variable name in the case pattern (`n` below) holds the matched value and is available inside the guard and the block.

```python
# Example 4: Guard Conditions for Range Checks

score = int(input("Enter exam score (0-100): "))

match score:
    case n if n < 0 or n > 100:
        print(f"Invalid score: {n}. Must be 0-100.")
    case n if n >= 90:
        print(f"Score {n}: Grade A -- Exceptional.")
    case n if n >= 75:
        print(f"Score {n}: Grade B -- Strong.")
    case n if n >= 60:
        print(f"Score {n}: Grade C -- Satisfactory.")
    case _:
        print(f"Score {score}: Grade F -- Failing.")
```

Expected Output

```
Enter exam score (0-100): 82
Score 82: Grade B -- Strong.
```

Example 5 -- Complete Program: Traffic Light Controller

This example brings together a string match, grouped values with |, and a wildcard fallback inside a complete interactive program. Read the header comment before tracing the logic.

```python
# ---------------------------------------------------
# Module   : traffic_controller.py
# Purpose  : Maps traffic light colour to driver action.
# Author   : Ayman Alzaid
# ---------------------------------------------------

light_colour = input("Enter light colour (red/amber/green): ").lower()

match light_colour:
    case "red":
        action = "STOP. Do not proceed."
    case "amber" | "yellow":  # accept both spellings
        action = "PREPARE. Light changing soon."
    case "green":
        action = "GO. Proceed when safe."
    case _:
        action = f"UNKNOWN colour: {light_colour}."

print(f"Signal: {light_colour.upper()}  >>  {action}")
```

Expected Output

```
Enter light colour (red/amber/green): amber
Signal: AMBER  >>  PREPARE. Light changing soon.
```

The Active Learning Framework

The three pillars below apply `match-case` against four specific behaviors: Pillar 1 traces the execution path through a guard-condition match statement. Pillar 2 presents four puzzles on fall-through assumptions, the wildcard behaviour, guard evaluation order, and the | operator. Pillar 3 audits a poorly written `if-elif` chain and refactors it into a clean `match-case` structure.

Active Learning Pillars: **P1** Trace the interpreter line by line. **P2** Predict the output before running. **P3** Audit and refactor to PEP 8 standards. Verify every prediction at the terminal.

Pillar 1 -- Logic Exercise: match-case Execution Trace

Tracing a `match` statement requires the same discipline as tracing an `if-elif` chain. Read the subject value, compare it against each case pattern from top to bottom, identify the first match, execute that block, and stop. Guard conditions add one extra step: the pattern must match *and* the guard must be True for the case to fire.

Trace Rule 1: The subject is evaluated once at the `match` line. **Trace Rule 2:** For plain value cases, fire if subject == pattern. **Trace Rule 3:** For guard cases, fire if pattern matches AND guard is True. **Trace Rule 4:** First match wins. All remaining cases are skipped.

PILLAR 1 Logic Exercise

Instructions: Using the variable value given in the script, trace the match statement one case at a time. Complete the Execution Path Table. Do not run the code.

Python

```
# Pillar 1: match-case Trace Exercise

sensor_reading = 72

match sensor_reading:
    case 0:
        print("Sensor offline.")
    case n if n < 0:
        print("Error: negative reading.")
    case n if n <= 50:
        print("Status: Normal range.")
    case n if n <= 80:
        print("Status: Elevated -- monitor closely.")
    case _:
        print("Alert: Critical reading!")
```

Execution Path Table

Case Evaluated	Pattern / Guard	Does it Match?	Action
case 0:	72 == 0	? fill in	? fires / skips
case n if n < 0:	72 < 0	? fill in	? fires / skips
case n if n <= 50:	72 <= 50	? fill in	? fires / skips
case n if n <= 80:	72 <= 80	? fill in	? fires / skips
case _:	always matches	not reached	not reached

Challenge Questions: Which case fires and what does it print? Why does `case n if n <= 50:` not fire even though n = 72 is a valid integer? What would the output be if sensor_reading were 0?

Pillar 2 -- Mysterious Output Puzzles: Predict Before You Run

Four puzzles test the edges of `match-case` behavior. The fall-through assumption from other languages, the wildcard capturing a value, guard evaluation interacting with the capture variable, and the | operator combined with `.lower()` preprocessing. Predict the exact output for every puzzle before running any code.

PILLAR 2 Mysterious Output Puzzles

Instructions: Predict the complete console output for each puzzle. Record all predictions before running anything. Then execute and compare.

Puzzle 6.1 -- The Fall-Through Assumption

Developers coming from C or JavaScript often assume that matched cases fall through into subsequent ones unless stopped. Python does not fall through. Predict exactly what prints and how many lines appear.

```python
# Puzzle 6.1: Does Python match-case fall through?

status = "active"

match status:
    case "active":
        print("Status: Active")
    case "active" | "running":
```

```
        print("System operational")
    case _:
        print("Unknown status")
```

Questions: How many lines print? Does "System operational" ever print? Why does the second case never fire even though "active" matches its pattern too?

Puzzle 6.2 -- The Wildcard Capture

The wildcard _ discards the matched value. But using a named variable in a case pattern *captures* it. Predict what prints and explain the difference between `case _:` and `case unknown_cmd:`.

```python
# Puzzle 6.2: Wildcard vs Named Capture

user_input = "launch"

match user_input:
    case "help":
        print("Showing help menu.")
    case unknown_cmd:  # captures the value
        print(f"No handler for: {unknown_cmd}")
```

Questions: What does this print? When the named capture `case unknown_cmd:` fires, what value does `unknown_cmd` hold? How is this different from `case _:`?

Puzzle 6.3 -- Guard Evaluation Order

Guards are evaluated only after their pattern matches. Predict the output for all three calls and identify which case fires for each value.

```python
# Puzzle 6.3: Guard Evaluation Order

def classify(n):
    match n:
        case n if n == 0:
            print("Zero")
        case n if n > 0:
```

```
            print(f"Positive: {n}")
        case _:
            print(f"Negative: {n}")

classify(5)
classify(0)
classify(-3)
```

Questions: What are the three outputs in order? For classify(-3), why does the first guard (n == 0) not fire? Why does the second guard (n > 0) not fire? Which case catches -3?

Puzzle 6.4 -- The | Operator and Preprocessing

The `.lower()` method converts a string to all lowercase before the match runs. Predict all three outputs and explain whether | would still be needed if the input were not preprocessed.

```python
# Puzzle 6.4: | Operator with Preprocessing

def check_yn(response):
    match response.lower():
        case "y" | "yes":
            print("Confirmed.")
        case "n" | "no":
            print("Cancelled.")
        case _:
            print(f"Invalid response: {response}")

check_yn("YES")
check_yn("No")
check_yn("maybe")
```

Questions: What are the three outputs? Without the `.lower()` call, would `"YES"` still match the first case? Why is | still needed even after lowercasing?

Pillar 3 -- Code Audit: Refactor if-elif to match-case

The script below uses an `if-elif` chain to route HTTP method strings. It contains four violations: repeated variable name in every condition, inconsistent capitalisation that breaks matching, a missing wildcard for unrecognised methods, and non-descriptive variable names. Record each violation, then refactor the entire script to a clean `match-case` structure.

PILLAR 3 Code Audit -- Refactor to match-case

Instructions: Identify every violation in the non-compliant script. Record each in the audit table. Then rewrite the complete script using match-case to production standards.

Non-Compliant Script

```python
m = input("HTTP method: ")

if m == "GET":
    print("Fetching resource")
elif m == "Post":  # BUG: wrong capitalisation
    print("Creating resource")
elif m == "PUT":
    print("Updating resource")
elif m == "DELETE":
    print("Deleting resource")
# BUG: no wildcard for unrecognised methods
```

#	Violation Found	Rule Broken	Corrected Pattern
1	Variable m -- single-letter, non-descriptive	Naming: use descriptive snake_case names	http_method = input(...)
2	"Post" uses wrong capitalisation -- will never match "POST"	Consistency: case patterns are case-sensitive. Use .upper() or standardise.	Normalise input: .upper() before match, or add | "Post" | "post"
3	No wildcard fallback -- unrecognised methods produce no output	Best practice: always include case _: in match-case for unexpected values	Add case _: with an error message
4	if-elif chain repeats m == on every line -- repetitive for single-variable routing	Style: when routing one variable against fixed values, match-case is cleaner	Refactor entire structure to match http_method:

Production-Quality Refactored Script

```python
# ------------------------------------------------
# Module  : http_router.py
# Purpose : Routes HTTP method strings to handler labels.
# Author  : Ayman Alzaid
# ------------------------------------------------

# .upper() normalises input so "get", "GET", "Get" all match
http_method = input("Enter HTTP method: ").upper()

match http_method:
    case "GET":
        print("GET -- Fetching resource.")
    case "POST":
        print("POST -- Creating resource.")
    case "PUT":
        print("PUT -- Updating resource.")
    case "DELETE":
        print("DELETE -- Removing resource.")
    case _:
        print(f"405 Method Not Allowed: {http_method}")
```

Coding Challenge: Currency Exchange Desk

Chapter 6 Coding Challenge

Objective: Build a currency exchange desk program that uses match-case to route currency codes and guard conditions to apply rate tiers. Every requirement below must appear in the solution.

>> Open with a PEP 8 compliant header comment block.

>> Collect two inputs: currency code (str) and amount to exchange (float).

>> Normalise the currency code using .upper() before the match statement.

>> Use match-case to apply exchange rates: USD = 3.75, EUR = 4.10, GBP = 4.80, JPY = 0.025. Group any alternative code spellings using |.

>> Add a guard condition case that detects if the amount is <= 0 before the currency cases and prints an error.

>> Include a wildcard case that reports the currency code as unsupported.

>> Print a formatted exchange receipt using f-strings showing input currency, amount, rate applied, and final converted value to 2 decimal places.

Chapter Summary

Concept	Key Takeaway
match-case	Evaluates a subject once and routes to the first matching case. Introduced in Python 3.10.
Version requirement	Python 3.10 or later. Raises SyntaxError on earlier versions.
One-path-wins	Same rule as if-elif: the first matching case executes and all others are skipped.
No fall-through	Python does not fall through to subsequent cases after a match. Each case is isolated.
case _:	Wildcard -- matches everything. Acts as the else fallback. Always place last.
| operator	Matches multiple values in one case clause. case "a" | "b": fires for either value.
Guard conditions	case n if n > 0: fires only when the pattern matches AND the guard is True.
Named capture	case unknown_val: captures the matched value into the variable for use inside the block.
When to use match-case	Best for routing one variable against specific fixed values: menus, commands, status codes.
When to use if-elif	Best for range checks, different variables per branch, or complex compound conditions.

CHAPTER 7

Functions in Python

Learning Objectives

1. Explain what a function is, why functions exist, and what problem they solve in software design.
2. Define a function using the def keyword with correct syntax, colon, and indentation.
3. Distinguish between parameters (definition) and arguments (call site) and explain how values are mapped at call time.
4. Use the return statement to send a computed value back to the calling scope.
5. Explain local scope: why variables declared inside a function are invisible to code outside it.
6. Define functions with default parameter values and call them with and without those arguments.
7. Use keyword arguments to pass values by name rather than by position.
8. Write a docstring to document a function's purpose, parameters, and return value.
9. Trace the full execution path of a function call: argument binding, local execution, and return value delivery.

Theoretical Foundation

The Problem Functions Solve

Every program written so far has been sequential: a flat list of statements executed from top to bottom. That model breaks down the moment a task needs to be performed more than once. Copying and pasting the same ten lines of code into three different places works once. The first time you find a bug in those ten lines, you must fix it in three places. Miss one and the program behaves inconsistently. Scale that to a hundred places and the codebase becomes unmaintainable.

A **function** solves this by giving a reusable block of code a name. Write the logic once, inside the function. Call it by name wherever it is needed. Fix a bug once, and the fix applies everywhere the function is called. This principle is called **DRY: Don't Repeat Yourself**. It is the foundation of every professional software architecture.

Functions also make programs readable. A script that reads:

```python
validate_input(user_data)
calculate_total(cart_items)
```

```
apply_discount(total, user_tier)
generate_receipt(final_price)
```

...communicates its intent in four lines. The reader understands the program's structure without reading a single implementation detail. Functions are not just a code-saving mechanism. They are the primary tool for expressing structure and intent.

Anatomy of a Function Definition

A function definition has four components. **The def keyword** opens the definition and tells Python that a function definition is starting. **The function name** follows immediately after `def`, using the same snake_case convention as all other identifiers. **The parameter list** sits inside parentheses after the name. It may be empty or contain one or more named placeholders. **The colon** ends the definition line and opens the indented block. Every line of the function's body is indented four spaces. The function does not execute when it is defined. It executes only when it is called.

Parameters vs Arguments

These two terms are frequently confused. They refer to the same values at different points in time. **Parameters** are the named placeholders in the function definition. They are declared when you write `def greet(name):`. The word `name` is a parameter. It does not hold a real value until the function is called.

Arguments are the actual values passed to the function at call time. When you write `greet("Alex")`, the string `"Alex"` is the argument. At the moment of the call, Python assigns the argument value to the parameter. Inside the function, `name` holds `"Alex"` for the duration of that call.

Term	Where It Lives	What It Contains	Example
Parameter	Function definition: def fn(x):	A named placeholder with no value yet	x in def add(x, y):
Argument	Function call: fn(10)	The actual value passed in at call time	10 in add(10, 5)

The return Statement

A function without a `return` statement performs actions but hands nothing back to the caller. A `print()` call inside a function displays text, but the text vanishes -- it is not stored or usable anywhere. The **return statement** is what allows a function to produce a value that the caller can store, use in further calculations, or pass to another function.

return has two effects: it sends the specified value back to the calling scope, and it immediately ends the function's execution. Any code written after a `return` statement in the same branch is unreachable and never runs. A function may have multiple `return` statements in different branches of a conditional, but only one will execute per call.

A function that has no `return` statement, or a `return` with no value, automatically returns `None`. Storing the result of such a function and attempting to use it in arithmetic will raise a `TypeError`.

Local Scope: The Function's Private Workspace

Every function call creates a private workspace called a **local scope**. Variables declared inside the function exist only within that scope. They are created when the function is called and destroyed when it returns. Code outside the function cannot read them, modify them, or even detect that they exist.

This isolation is not a limitation. It is a feature. Local scope means a function cannot accidentally interfere with variables in the calling code. You can name a parameter `total` inside a function even if a variable named `total` already exists outside. They are entirely separate. The function's `total` does not touch the outer `total`.

Figure 7.1 -- Function Call: Arguments, Local Scope, and Return

The diagram below shows the full journey of a function call. Arguments travel from the calling scope into the function's local workspace. The local variable `total` exists only inside the function. The return value travels back and is stored by the caller.

	Calling Scope		Function Scope (local)		
	result = add(3, 5) arguments: 3, 5	>> **args** >>	**def add(a, b):** total = a + b return total parameters: a=3, b=5	**<< return <<**	
	result receives 8		*total is local -- invisible outside*		

Default Parameter Values

A parameter can be given a **default value** in the function definition. If the caller does not provide an argument for that parameter, the default is used automatically. If the caller does provide an argument, the provided value overrides the default.

Parameters with defaults must always appear *after* parameters without defaults in the definition. Writing `def fn(x=5, y):` raises a `SyntaxError`. Python cannot determine which argument corresponds to which parameter if a required parameter follows an optional one.

Keyword Arguments

Normally, arguments are matched to parameters by **position**: the first argument goes to the first parameter, and so on. Python also supports **keyword arguments**, where the caller explicitly names the parameter being assigned. Writing `greet(name="Alex", title="Dr.")` maps each value by name rather than position. Keyword arguments can be passed in any order, and they make function calls self-documenting.

Docstrings: Documenting Your Functions

A **docstring** is a string literal placed as the very first statement inside a function body. It documents the function's purpose, its parameters, and its return value. It is enclosed in triple quotes (`"""`) and is accessible at runtime via `help()` and `.__doc__`. PEP 257 defines the convention: one summary line, then a blank line, then detailed description if needed.

Formal Syntax and Declaration

Function Definition Syntax

```python
# Function Definition -- Formal Syntax

def function_name(param_one, param_two):
    """Docstring: what this function does."""
    # function body -- indented 4 spaces
    local_variable = param_one + param_two
    return local_variable

# Function Call -- arguments bound to parameters by position
result = function_name(10, 20)
```

Component	Syntax	Required?	Notes
def keyword	def	Yes	Always first. Signals a function definition to the interpreter.
Function name	snake_case	Yes	Same naming rules as variables. Should describe what the function does.
Parentheses	()	Yes	Must be present even if empty. Parameters listed inside.
Colon	:	Yes	Ends the definition line. Omitting it raises SyntaxError.
Docstring	"""..."""	Recommended	First statement inside the body. Documents purpose and parameters.
return	return value	No	Without return, the function returns None automatically.

Default Parameters and Keyword Arguments

```python
# Default parameters -- defaults must come AFTER required params
def greet(name, title="User", formal=False):
    """Return a greeting string."""
    if formal:
        return f"Good day, {title} {name}."
    return f"Hello, {name}!"

# Positional call -- title and formal use defaults
print(greet("Alex"))                          # Hello, Alex!

# Keyword call -- arguments by name, any order
print(greet(formal=True, name="Smith", title="Dr."))  # Good day, Dr. Smith.
```

Implementation and Code Examples

Example 1 -- Defining and Calling a Function

The simplest useful function: one parameter, one computation, one return value. Notice that the function is defined first and called second. Python must read the definition before it can execute a call to it.

```python
# Example 1: Define, Call, Receive Return Value

def square(number):
    """Return the square of a number."""
    return number ** 2

# Call the function and store the return value
result_a = square(5)    # 5 ** 2 = 25
result_b = square(12)  # 12 ** 2 = 144

print(f"Square of 5:  {result_a}")
print(f"Square of 12: {result_b}")
```

Expected Output

```
Square of 5:  25
Square of 12: 144
```

Example 2 -- Multiple Parameters and Local Scope

This example demonstrates two key concepts simultaneously. The function receives two arguments, maps them to two parameters, and computes a local result. The variable `area` inside the function is local: it does not exist outside. Only the return value crosses the boundary back into the calling scope.

```python
# Example 2: Multiple Parameters and Local Variables

def calculate_area(length, width):
    """Return area of a rectangle."""
    area = length * width  # local variable -- invisible outside
    return area

room_area = calculate_area(5.0, 3.5)
print(f"Room area: {room_area} sq metres")

# Attempting to access local variable here would raise NameError:
# print(area)  <-- NameError: name 'area' is not defined
```

Expected Output

```
Room area: 17.5 sq metres
```

Example 3 -- Default Parameter Values

Default values make parameters optional at the call site. The caller may override any default by providing an explicit argument. Read each of the three calls below and trace which default is used and which is overridden.

```python
# Example 3: Default Parameter Values
```

```
def format_price(amount, currency="USD", decimals=2):
    """Format a price with currency and decimal precision."""
    return f"{currency} {amount:.{decimals}f}"

# Call 1: only required argument -- both defaults apply
print(format_price(19.99))                      # USD 19.99

# Call 2: override currency -- decimals default applies
print(format_price(49.5, "EUR"))                # EUR 49.50

# Call 3: override both defaults
print(format_price(1250.0, "GBP", 0))          # GBP 1250
```

Expected Output
USD 19.99
EUR 49.50
GBP 1250

Example 4 -- Keyword Arguments and Docstrings

Keyword arguments remove the need to remember parameter order. They make long function calls self-documenting and less error-prone. The docstring below follows PEP 257: a one-line summary, then a blank line, then parameter descriptions.

```
Python
# Example 4: Keyword Arguments and PEP 257 Docstring

def build_profile(username, age, role="student"):
    """Build and return a user profile dictionary.

    Args:
        username (str): The account display name.
        age (int): User age in whole years.
        role (str): Account role. Defaults to "student".

    Returns:
        dict: A dictionary of the user's profile data.
```

```
    """
    return {"username": username, "age": age, "role": role}

# Positional call
p1 = build_profile("alex99", 22)
print(p1)

# Keyword call -- order does not matter
p2 = build_profile(age=35, role="admin", username="jsmith")
print(p2)
```

Expected Output

```
{'username': 'alex99', 'age': 22, 'role': 'student'}
{'username': 'jsmith', 'age': 35, 'role': 'admin'}
```

Example 5 -- Complete Program: Invoice Calculator

This example builds a small system from three cooperating functions. Each function does one clearly defined job. The main logic calls them in sequence, passing return values forward. This is the function-based architecture style used throughout professional Python.

Python

```
# ---------------------------------------------------
# Module  : invoice_calculator.py
# Purpose : Computes invoice total using modular functions.
# Author  : Ayman Alzaid
# ---------------------------------------------------

def get_subtotal(price, quantity):
    """Return subtotal: price multiplied by quantity."""
    return price * quantity

def apply_tax(subtotal, rate=0.08):
    """Return total after applying a tax rate. Default rate 8%."""
    return subtotal * (1 + rate)

def print_invoice(item, price, qty, tax_rate=0.08):
    """Print a formatted invoice to the console."""
```

```
    subtotal = get_subtotal(price, qty)
    total    = apply_tax(subtotal, tax_rate)
    print(f"Item:     {item}")
    print(f"Subtotal: ${subtotal:.2f}")
    print(f"Tax ({tax_rate*100:.0f}%):  ${total - subtotal:.2f}")
    print(f"Total:    ${total:.2f}")

print_invoice("Python Textbook", 49.99, 3)
```

Expected Output

```
Item:     Python Textbook
Subtotal: $149.97
Tax (8%):  $12.00
Total:    $161.97
```

The Active Learning Framework

The three pillars below test function mechanics directly. Pillar 1 requires tracing a complete function call including argument binding, local scope, and return value delivery. Pillar 2 presents four puzzles targeting return vs print confusion, scope errors, default parameter mutation, and None returns. Pillar 3 audits a common beginner function with five violations.

Active Learning Pillars: **P1** Trace the interpreter line by line. **P2** Predict the output before running. **P3** Audit and refactor to PEP 8 standards. Verify every prediction at the terminal.

Pillar 1 -- Logic Exercise: Function Call Trace

Tracing a function call adds a new layer to the interpreter trace technique. When the interpreter reaches a function call, execution jumps into the function body. Arguments are bound to parameters. The local scope is created. When `return` is reached, the return value is delivered to the call site and the local scope is destroyed.

Trace Rule 1: At the call site, substitute each argument into its matching parameter by position. **Trace Rule 2:** Local variables exist only inside the function. Record them separately from outer variables. **Trace Rule 3:** When return executes, record the value delivered back to the caller and mark the local scope destroyed. **Trace Rule 4:** Code after return in the same branch never executes.

PILLAR 1 Logic Exercise

Instructions: Trace the script below one step at a time. Complete the full Call Trace Table. Record argument binding, all local variables, the return value, and the final state of outer variables. Do not run the code.

```python
# Pillar 1: Function Call Trace Exercise

def process(x, y, multiplier=2):
    total  = x + y
    result = total * multiplier
    return result

alpha = 6
beta  = 4
output = process(alpha, beta)        # Call 1: default multiplier
print(output)

output = process(alpha, beta, 5)  # Call 2: explicit multiplier
print(output)
```

Function Call Trace Table

Step	Action	Local: x	Local: y	Local: multiplier	Local: total	Local: result	Outer: output
Call 1 enters	process(6, 4)	6	4	2 (default)	?	?	not yet
total = x + y	compute total	6	4	2	? compute	?	not yet
result = total * multiplier	compute result	6	4	2	10	? compute	not yet
return result	deliver to caller	--	--	--	destroyed	destroyed	? fill in
print(output)	display						? fill in
Call 2 enters	process(6, 4, 5)	6	4	5	?	?	not yet
return result	deliver to caller	--	--	--	destroyed	destroyed	? fill in
print(output)	display						? fill in

Challenge Questions: What are the two printed values? Why does changing multiplier in Call 2 not affect alpha or beta? What happens to the local variable total after return executes?

Pillar 2 -- Mysterious Output Puzzles: Predict Before You Run

Four puzzles test the edges of function behavior. The return vs print confusion, the scope isolation rule, the None return trap, and the unexpected behavior when a default argument is a mutable object. Predict the exact console output for every puzzle before running anything.

PILLAR 2 Mysterious Output Puzzles

Instructions: Predict the complete console output for each puzzle. Record all predictions before running anything. Then execute and compare.

Puzzle 7.1 -- The return vs print Trap

Two functions look almost identical. One uses `return`, the other uses `print` inside the body. Predict all four lines of output and explain why storing the result of the second function produces `None`.

```python
# Puzzle 7.1: return vs print

def double_return(n):
    return n * 2

def double_print(n):
    print(n * 2)

a = double_return(5)
b = double_print(5)

print(a)
print(b)
```

Questions: How many total lines appear on the console and in what order? Why does `b` hold `None`? Which of the two functions is useful when you need to do further arithmetic with the result?

Puzzle 7.2 -- The Scope Boundary

Local variables do not leak out of functions. Predict what this script prints and identify the exact line that would crash if the comment were removed.

```python
# Puzzle 7.2: Scope Boundary

score = 100  # outer variable

def update_score(points):
    score = points + 50  # local variable -- shadows outer score
    return score

new_score = update_score(30)
print(new_score)
print(score)      # which score is this?
```

Questions: What are the two printed values? The outer `score` is 100. Inside the function, `score` is assigned 80. After the function returns, what does the outer `score` hold and why?

Puzzle 7.3 -- The None Arithmetic Crash

This script attempts to use a function's return value in a calculation. Predict whether it runs successfully or crashes, and if it crashes, identify the exact line and error type.

```python
# Puzzle 7.3: None Return in Arithmetic

def show_total(a, b):
    total = a + b
    print(f"Total: {total}")
    # No return statement

result = show_total(10, 5)
final  = result + 100
print(final)
```

Questions: Does the script produce any output before it crashes? What is the exact error type on the crash line? What one-word addition to the function definition would fix the problem?

Puzzle 7.4 -- The Default Value Trap

Default parameter values in Python are evaluated *once at definition time*, not on each call. For immutable defaults like integers and strings this makes no difference. Predict what this script prints and explain why the output is surprising.

```
Python

# Puzzle 7.4: Mutable Default Argument

def add_item(item, cart=[]):
    """Add item to cart list and return cart."""
    cart.append(item)
    return cart

order_1 = add_item("apple")
order_2 = add_item("bread")

print(order_1)
print(order_2)
```

Questions: Most students predict ['apple'] and ['bread']. What does the script actually print? Why does order_1 contain both items even though only "apple" was passed to that call? What is the standard Python fix for this class of bug?

Pillar 3 -- Code Audit: Function Design Violations

The function below attempts to calculate a discounted price. It contains five violations: a missing docstring, a non-descriptive parameter name, a return vs print confusion that makes the function useless to its caller, a hardcoded magic number with no explanation, and a non-descriptive function name. Identify every violation, record each in the audit table, and rewrite to production standards.

PILLAR 3 Code Audit -- Function Design

Instructions: Identify every violation in the non-compliant function. Record each in the table. Then rewrite the complete function to production standards.

Non-Compliant Function

```python
def calc(x, y):
    z = x - (x * 0.15)  # 0.15 unexplained magic number
    print(z)            # should return, not print
```

#	Violation Found	Rule Broken	Corrected Pattern
1	No docstring	PEP 257: all functions should have a docstring describing purpose, params, and return	Add """Return discounted price..."""
2	Function name calc is non-descriptive	Naming: function names must describe what they do	calculate_discounted_price
3	Parameters x and y are single-letter and meaningless	Naming: parameters must describe the data they receive	price, discount_rate
4	Magic number 0.15 with no explanation	Clarity: hardcoded values must be named constants or explained via parameter	Use discount_rate parameter with a default
5	print(z) instead of return z	Design: use return so the caller can store and reuse the result	return discounted_price

Production-Quality Refactored Function

```python
def calculate_discounted_price(price, discount_rate=0.15):
    """Return the price after applying a percentage discount.

    Args:
        price (float): The original item price.
        discount_rate (float): Discount as a decimal. Defaults to 0.15 (15%).

    Returns:
        float: The price after discount.
    """
    discount_amount    = price * discount_rate
    discounted_price   = price - discount_amount
    return discounted_price

# Caller stores the return value and uses it further
final_price = calculate_discounted_price(120.00)
```

```
print(f"Discounted price: ${final_price:.2f}")
```

Coding Challenge: Student Grade Report Builder

Chapter 7 Coding Challenge

Objective: Build a modular student grade report system using multiple cooperating functions. Every requirement below must be satisfied.

>> Open with a PEP 8 compliant header comment block.

>> Write a function get_grade(score) that accepts a score (int) and returns the letter grade string using an if-elif-else chain: A (>=90), B (>=80), C (>=70), D (>=60), F (below 60).

>> Write a function calculate_average(scores) that accepts a list of numbers and returns the average. Use the built-in sum() and len() functions.

>> Write a function is_passing(average, threshold=60.0) that returns True if the average meets the threshold, False otherwise.

>> Write a function print_report(student_name, scores) that calls the three functions above and prints a formatted report: student name, all scores, calculated average, letter grade, and pass/fail status.

>> Call print_report at least twice with different student data to verify all branches work correctly.

>> Add a PEP 257 docstring to every function.

Chapter Summary

Concept	Key Takeaway
Function purpose	Write logic once, call it anywhere. Eliminates repetition and makes code readable.
def keyword	Opens a function definition. Followed by name, parentheses, parameters, and colon.
Parameters	Named placeholders in the function definition. Have no value until the function is called.
Arguments	Actual values passed at the call site. Bound to parameters by position (or by name with keyword args).
return statement	Sends a value back to the calling scope and ends the function immediately.
None return	A function without return, or return with no value, automatically returns None. Using None in arithmetic raises TypeError.
Local scope	Variables declared inside a function exist only for the duration of that call. They are invisible outside.
Default parameters	Assign a default value in the definition. The caller may override or omit. Defaults are evaluated once at definition time.
Keyword arguments	Pass arguments by name: fn(param=value). Order does not matter. Self-documenting.
Docstring	Triple-quoted string as the first statement inside the body. Documents purpose, params, and return value.
Mutable default trap	Never use a mutable object (list, dict) as a default argument. Use None and assign inside the body.

C H A P T E R 8

Python's Built-in Functions and High-Quality Coding Standards

Learning Objectives

1. Explain what built-in functions are and why they require no import statement.
2. Apply type conversion functions (int, float, str, bool) to transform values between data types.
3. Use numeric utility functions (abs, round, pow, divmod, min, max, sum) to perform common mathematical operations.
4. Use introspection functions (type, len, id, isinstance) to inspect values and enforce type safety.
5. Apply sequence tools (range, sorted, enumerate, zip, reversed) to work with ordered collections.
6. Predict the output of built-in functions applied to edge-case inputs.
7. Apply all major PEP 8 rules: naming conventions, whitespace, line length, import order, and comment standards.
8. Audit a non-compliant script and refactor it to meet every PEP 8 requirement.

Theoretical Foundation

Python's Built-in Toolkit

Python ships with more than 70 built-in functions that are always available in every Python script without any import statement. They are part of the language itself. Every program written in the previous seven chapters has used at least three: `print()`, `input()`, and `int()` or `float()`. Most beginners use these instinctively without realising they represent a larger, organized toolkit.

Knowing the full set of built-ins is a mark of Python fluency. A programmer who reaches for a built-in solves the problem in one readable line. A programmer who does not know it exists writes ten lines to do the same thing, introduces bugs, and creates maintenance burden. The goal of this chapter is to eliminate that gap.

Figure 8.1 -- Built-in Function Categories

The 22 most essential built-ins are organized into five categories below. All are available immediately in any Python 3 script.

Python Built-in Functions -- Always Available, No Import Needed

Type Conversion	Numeric Utilities	Introspection	Sequence Tools	I/O
`int()` `float()` `str()` `bool()`	`abs()` `round()` `pow()` `divmod()` `min()` `max()` `sum()`	`type()` `len()` `id()` `isinstance()` `help()`	`range()` `sorted()` `enumerate()` `zip()` `reversed()`	`print()` `input()`

Python 3 provides 68 built-in functions. This chapter covers the 22 most essential for everyday programming.

PEP 8: The Professional Coding Standard

Previous chapters introduced PEP 8 rules as they became relevant. This chapter consolidates them into a complete reference. **PEP 8** (Python Enhancement Proposal 8) is the official style guide for Python code. It was written by Guido van Rossum, the creator of Python, and defines the conventions that make Python code readable across teams, organizations, and years of maintenance.

PEP 8 compliance is not optional in professional environments. Code submitted for review in most software teams is automatically checked against PEP 8 using tools like `flake8` and `pylint`. A violation stops the review process until the style issue is fixed. Developing PEP 8 habits now means writing code that is accepted immediately without revision cycles.

Built-in Functions: Complete Reference

Category 1 -- Type Conversion Functions

These functions construct a new object of the target type from the given value. They do not modify the original. They produce and return a new object.

Function	Input	Returns	Notes and Edge Cases
int(x)	str, float, bool	Integer	int("42") = 42. int(3.9) truncates to 3. int("7.5") raises ValueError.
float(x)	str, int, bool	Float	float("3.14") = 3.14. float(True) = 1.0.
str(x)	Any type	String	str(100) = "100". str(None) = "None". Always safe -- never raises ValueError.
bool(x)	Any type	Boolean	False for 0, 0.0, "", [], None. True for everything else.

Category 2 -- Numeric Utility Functions

These functions perform common mathematical operations that would otherwise require manual formulas. Using them is faster and less error-prone than writing the equivalent arithmetic.

<table>
<tr><th>Function</th><th>Signature</th><th>Returns</th><th>Example</th></tr>
<tr><td>abs()</td><td>abs(x)</td><td>Absolute value</td><td>abs(-7) = 7 | abs(-3.5) = 3.5</td></tr>
<tr><td>round()</td><td>round(x, n=0)</td><td>Rounded float or int</td><td>round(3.7) = 4 | round(3.145, 2) = 3.14</td></tr>
<tr><td>pow()</td><td>pow(base, exp)</td><td>base raised to exp</td><td>pow(2, 10) = 1024 | equivalent to 2 ** 10</td></tr>
<tr><td>divmod()</td><td>divmod(a, b)</td><td>Tuple (quotient, remainder)</td><td>divmod(17, 5) = (3, 2) | same as (17//5, 17%5)</td></tr>
<tr><td>min()</td><td>min(a, b, ...)</td><td>Smallest value</td><td>min(4, 1, 9, 2) = 1 | min("apple", "fig") = "apple"</td></tr>
<tr><td>max()</td><td>max(a, b, ...)</td><td>Largest value</td><td>max(4, 1, 9, 2) = 9</td></tr>
<tr><td>sum()</td><td>sum(iterable)</td><td>Total of all elements</td><td>sum([10, 20, 30]) = 60 | requires an iterable</td></tr>
</table>

Category 3 -- Introspection Functions

Introspection functions reveal information about a value at runtime. They answer questions like: what type is this? How many elements does it have? Is it an instance of a particular class?

<table>
<tr><th>Function</th><th>Signature</th><th>Returns</th><th>Example</th></tr>
<tr><td>type()</td><td>type(x)</td><td>The class of x</td><td>type(42) = <class 'int'> | type('hi') = <class 'str'></td></tr>
<tr><td>len()</td><td>len(x)</td><td>Number of elements</td><td>len("hello") = 5 | len([1,2,3]) = 3 | len({}) = 0</td></tr>
<tr><td>id()</td><td>id(x)</td><td>Memory address (integer)</td><td>id(x) returns a unique integer for the object x refers to</td></tr>
<tr><td>isinstance()</td><td>isinstance(x, T)</td><td>True if x is instance of T</td><td>isinstance(42, int) = True | isinstance("hi", int) = False</td></tr>
</table>

isinstance() vs type(): Which to Use

Use isinstance(): isinstance(x, int) returns True for integers and also for subclasses of int. This is the recommended approach in production code.

Use type() == when: you need exact type matching and do not want subclasses to pass. type(x) == int is True only if x is exactly an int, not a subclass.

Practical rule: isinstance() for validation, type() for inspection and debugging.

Category 4 -- Sequence and Iteration Tools

These functions transform, sort, or navigate ordered sequences. They are covered in detail when lists and loops appear in Chapters 9 through 12. This reference introduces their signatures and key behaviors as preparation.

Function	Signature	Returns	Key Behavior
range()	range(stop) or range(start, stop, step)	Range object	Generates integers. range(5) = 0,1,2,3,4. Used in for loops.
sorted()	sorted(iterable, reverse=False)	New sorted list	Does not modify the original. Returns a new sorted list.
reversed()	reversed(sequence)	Iterator (reversed)	Returns an iterator. Wrap in list() to see values.
enumerate()	enumerate(iterable, start=0)	Iterator of (index, value) pairs	Provides index and value together. Essential in loops.
zip()	zip(iter1, iter2, ...)	Iterator of tuples	Pairs elements from multiple sequences. Stops at shortest.

PEP 8: High-Quality Coding Standards

The rules below consolidate every PEP 8 convention introduced across Chapters 1 through 7 and add the remaining conventions a professional Python developer applies consistently.

Naming Conventions

Identifier Type	Convention	Correct	Incorrect
Variables and functions	lowercase_snake_case	player_score, get_total()	PlayerScore, getTotal(), x
Constants	ALL_CAPS_SNAKE_CASE	MAX_RETRIES, TAX_RATE	maxRetries, tax_rate
Classes	CapWords (PascalCase)	BankAccount, UserProfile	bank_account, userprofile
Private/internal	Leading underscore: _name	_helper(), _cache	helper(), cache (no signal)
Boolean variables	Affirmative question form	is_active, has_permission	active, permission, flag

Whitespace Rules

Rule	Incorrect	Correct
One space each side of = in assignments	x=10	x = 10
One space each side of arithmetic operators	total=price+tax	total = price + tax
No space inside parentheses	print(x)	print(x)
No space before colon in slice/dict	my_dict [key]	my_dict[key]
Two blank lines between top-level functions	def a(): ... def b(): ...	def a(): ... def b(): ...
One blank line between methods inside a class	(methods run together)	One blank line between each method

Line Length, Imports, and Comments

Rule	Standard	Notes
Maximum line length	79 characters	Use backslash \ or parentheses to wrap long lines.
Import order	Standard library, then third-party, then local	One import per line. Blank line between each group.
Import style	import module or from module import name	Never use: from module import *
Inline comments	# Two spaces before #, one space after #	score += 1 # increment score
Block comments	Full sentence, period at end.	# Calculate the final invoice total.
Docstrings	Triple quotes on functions, classes, modules	PEP 257: one-line summary, blank line, then detail.
No trailing whitespace	Remove all spaces at end of lines	Most editors do this automatically -- check settings.

Implementation and Code Examples

Example 1 -- Numeric Utilities in Practice

These six built-in functions replace custom arithmetic that beginners frequently write from scratch. Study the output of each call and confirm it matches the function's definition in the reference table above.

```python
# Example 1: Numeric Utility Functions

readings = [-12.5, 7.3, -0.8, 45.1, 3.0]

# abs() -- removes the sign
print(abs(-12.5))              # 12.5

# min() and max() -- across multiple arguments
print(min(-12.5, 7.3, -0.8, 45.1, 3.0))  # -12.5
print(max(-12.5, 7.3, -0.8, 45.1, 3.0))  # 45.1

# round() -- control decimal precision
average = sum(readings) / len(readings)
print(f"Average: {round(average, 2)}")  # Average: 8.42

# divmod() -- quotient AND remainder in one call
quotient, remainder = divmod(17, 5)
print(f"17 / 5 = {quotient} remainder {remainder}")
```

Expected Output
12.5
-12.5
45.1
Average: 8.42
17 / 5 = 3 remainder 2

Example 2 -- Introspection and Type Safety

This example demonstrates using `type()`, `isinstance()`, and `len()` to inspect values before operating on them. Checking types before arithmetic prevents `TypeError` crashes on unexpected input.

```
Python

# Example 2: Introspection Functions

def safe_double(value):
    """Double a value only if it is numeric; otherwise return an error string."""
    if isinstance(value, (int, float)):
        return value * 2
    return f"Error: {type(value).__name__} is not numeric"

print(safe_double(21))          # 42
print(safe_double(3.5))         # 7.0
print(safe_double("hello"))    # Error: str is not numeric

# len() counts elements in any sequence
message = "Python"
print(f"Length of {message!r}: {len(message)}")  # 6
```

Expected Output
42
7.0
Error: str is not numeric
Length of 'Python': 6

Example 3 -- Sequence Tools: sorted, enumerate, zip

These three functions transform how you interact with sequences. `sorted()` produces an ordered copy. `enumerate()` adds index numbers. `zip()` pairs matching elements from two sequences. All three return iterators -- wrap them in `list()` to see their contents outside a loop.

```
Python

# Example 3: sorted(), enumerate(), zip()

names  = ["Ellie", "Fatima", "Hadi"]
```

```
scores = [88, 95, 72]

# sorted() -- new list, original unchanged
print(sorted(names))                    # alphabetical
print(sorted(scores, reverse=True))         # descending

# enumerate() -- index + value pairs
for rank, name in enumerate(sorted(names), start=1):
    print(f"{rank}. {name}")

# zip() -- pair names with scores
paired = list(zip(names, scores))
print(paired)
```

Expected Output

```
['Fatima', 'Hadi', 'Ellie']
[95, 88, 72]
1. Fatima
2. Hadi
3. Ellie
[('Ellie', 88), ('Fatima', 95), ('Hadi', 72)]
```

Example 4 -- bool() and Truthy/Falsy Values

Python evaluates any value as True or False in a Boolean context. Values that evaluate to `False` are called **falsy**: `0`, `0.0`, `""`, `[]`, `None`. Everything else is **truthy**. The `bool()` function makes this evaluation explicit.

```
Python
# Example 4: bool() and Truthy/Falsy Values

# Falsy values -- all evaluate to False
print(bool(0))          # False -- zero integer
print(bool(""))         # False -- empty string
print(bool([]))         # False -- empty list
print(bool(None))       # False -- None
```

```
# Truthy values -- everything non-zero / non-empty
print(bool(1))         # True
print(bool("hello"))   # True
print(bool(-99))       # True -- any non-zero number
```

Expected Output
False
False
False
False
True
True
True

Example 5 -- Complete Program: Student Statistics Calculator

This example uses eight built-in functions inside a PEP 8 compliant module. Read the header comment, the docstring, and every inline comment before tracing the logic.

```
Python
# --------------------------------------------------
# Module  : student_stats.py
# Purpose : Computes and displays statistics for a
#           student score list using built-in functions.
# Author  : Ayman Alzaid
# --------------------------------------------------

def summarise_scores(scores):
    """Print a statistical summary of a list of scores.

    Args:
        scores (list): A list of numeric scores.
    """
    count   = len(scores)               # number of entries
    total   = sum(scores)               # sum of all scores
    average = round(total / count, 1)   # mean to 1 dp
    highest = max(scores)
```

```
    lowest   = min(scores)
    ranked   = sorted(scores, reverse=True)

    print(f"Count:    {count}")
    print(f"Average: {average}")
    print(f"Highest: {highest}")
    print(f"Lowest:  {lowest}")
    print(f"Ranked:  {ranked}")

class_scores = [78, 92, 65, 88, 73, 97, 84]
summarise_scores(class_scores)
```

Expected Output

```
Count:    7
Average: 82.4
Highest: 97
Lowest:  65
Ranked:  [97, 92, 88, 84, 78, 73, 65]
```

Combining Built-ins with User-Defined Functions

Chapter 7 established how to define functions. This chapter established what built-in tools are available. In well-written Python, these two things work together. A well-designed function calls built-ins internally to do the heavy lifting, keeping its own logic focused on structure and intent rather than low-level computation. The three patterns below demonstrate how this integration looks in practice.

Pattern 1 -- Numeric Built-ins Inside a Calculation Function

The most common pattern: a user-defined function that accepts a dataset and uses `sum()`, `len()`, `round()`, `min()`, and `max()` to produce a structured result. The caller does not need to know which built-ins were used. It simply calls the function and receives a clean, computed answer.

```
Python
# Pattern 1: Numeric Built-ins Inside a Function

def analyse_scores(scores):
```

```
    """Return a summary dict using numeric built-ins."""
    return {
        "count"  : len(scores),
        "total"  : sum(scores),
        "average": round(sum(scores) / len(scores), 2),
        "highest": max(scores),
        "lowest" : min(scores),
    }

results = analyse_scores([72, 88, 95, 61, 84, 77])
for key, value in results.items():
    print(f"{key:10}: {value}")
```

Expected Output

```
count      : 6
total      : 477
average    : 79.5
highest    : 95
lowest     : 61
```

Pattern 2 -- isinstance() as an Input Guard

A function that receives input from outside its own scope cannot trust that input. The caller may pass a string where a number is expected, or an empty list where elements are required. `isinstance()` and `len()` placed at the top of a function create a validation gate. If the input fails the check, the function exits early with a clear error message. This prevents obscure crashes deep inside the function logic and makes the error immediately actionable.

```python
# Pattern 2: isinstance() and len() as Input Guards

def calculate_average(values):
    """Return the average of a non-empty numeric list."""
    # Guard 1: must be a list
    if not isinstance(values, list):
        return "Error: input must be a list."
    # Guard 2: must not be empty
    if len(values) == 0:
```

```
        return "Error: list cannot be empty."
    # Guard 3: all elements must be numeric
    if not all(isinstance(v, (int, float)) for v in values):
        return "Error: all elements must be int or float."
    # All guards passed -- safe to compute
    return round(sum(values) / len(values), 2)

print(calculate_average([10, 20, 30]))          # 20.0
print(calculate_average("hello"))           # Error: input must be a list.
print(calculate_average([]))                 # Error: list cannot be empty.
print(calculate_average([10, "x", 30]))      # Error: all elements must be int or float.
```

Expected Output
20.0
Error: input must be a list.
Error: list cannot be empty.
Error: all elements must be int or float.

Pattern 3 -- Sequence Tools Powering Structured Output

The third pattern wraps `sorted()`, `enumerate()`, and `zip()` inside a function to produce a structured, readable report from two raw data lists. The caller provides names and scores. The function handles all ordering, pairing, and formatting internally. The result is clean, predictable output produced by a single function call.

```
Python
# Pattern 3: Sequence Tools Inside a Report Function

def print_leaderboard(names, scores):
    """Print a ranked leaderboard from two parallel lists."""
    # zip() pairs each name with its score
    paired  = list(zip(names, scores))

    # sorted() orders by score descending -- key=lambda unpacks the tuple
    ranked  = sorted(paired, key=lambda x: x[1], reverse=True)

    # enumerate() adds rank numbers starting at 1
    print("Rank   Name           Score")
```

```
    print("-" * 26)
    for rank, (name, score) in enumerate(ranked, start=1):
        print(f"{rank:<6} {name:<12} {score:>6}")

student_names  = ["Fatima", "Hadi", "Ellie", "Diana"]
student_scores = [88, 72, 95, 81]
print_leaderboard(student_names, student_scores)
```

Expected Output

```
Rank   Name          Score
--------------------------
1      Ellie           95
2      Fatima             88
3      Diana            81
4      Hadi               72
```

The Professional Pattern: Built-ins Inside Functions

Rule: User-defined functions provide structure, naming, and intent. Built-in functions provide computation. Combine them: the function defines what to do, the built-ins handle how to compute it.

Always: Place isinstance() and len() guards at the top of any function that receives external input. This eliminates cryptic crashes and makes error messages immediately useful.

Never: Write a manual loop to compute a sum, count elements, or find a minimum. sum(), len(), min(), max() already exist. Using them is faster, shorter, and more readable.

The Active Learning Framework

The three pillars below apply built-in functions and PEP 8 standards on the most common built-in edge cases. Pillar 1 traces a script that chains several built-in calls. Pillar 2 presents four puzzles on divmod unpacking, bool edge cases, sorted immutability, and isinstance with tuples. Pillar 3 audits a non-compliant script with six violations.

> **Active Learning Pillars:** **P1** Trace the interpreter line by line. **P2** Predict the output before running. **P3** Audit and refactor to PEP 8 standards. Verify every prediction at the terminal.

Pillar 1 -- Logic Exercise: Built-in Chain Trace

Tracing a script that chains built-in calls requires evaluating each function from the inside out. When a built-in appears as an argument to another function, the inner call evaluates first. Resolve each nested call in order and record the intermediate value before moving to the outer call.

Trace Rule 1: Evaluate innermost function calls first. **Trace Rule 2:** divmod() returns a tuple: (quotient, remainder). When unpacked, the first variable receives quotient and the second receives remainder. **Trace Rule 3:** round(x, n) rounds to n decimal places. round(x) with no second argument rounds to the nearest integer.

PILLAR 1 Logic Exercise

Instructions: Trace the script below one line at a time. Complete the Execution Trace Table. Record the exact value and type of every variable after each assignment. Do not run the code.

```python
# Pillar 1: Built-in Chain Trace Exercise

data = [5, 12, 3, 8, 7, 1]

total    = sum(data)
count    = len(data)
mean     = round(total / count, 2)
q, r     = divmod(total, count)
top_3    = sorted(data, reverse=True)[:3]
is_valid = isinstance(mean, float)

print(total, count, mean, q, r, top_3, is_valid)
```

Execution Trace Table

Variable	Expression Evaluated	Value	Type
total	sum([5,12,3,8,7,1])	? compute	int
count	len([5,12,3,8,7,1])	? compute	int
mean	round(total/count, 2)	? compute	float
q, r	divmod(total, count)	? two values	int, int
top_3	sorted(data, reverse=True)[:3]	? list	list
is_valid	isinstance(mean, float)	? fill in	bool

Challenge Questions: What does the final print statement display on one line? Why is mean a float even though total and count are both integers? What does [:3] do to the sorted list?

Pillar 2 -- Mysterious Output Puzzles: Predict Before You Run

Four puzzles test the edges of built-in function behavior. The divmod unpacking pattern, the surprising results of bool() on unexpected inputs, the immutability of sorted() on the original sequence, and isinstance() accepting a tuple of types. Predict every output before running anything.

PILLAR 2 Mysterious Output Puzzles

Instructions: Predict the complete console output for each puzzle. Record all predictions before running. Then execute and compare.

Puzzle 8.1 -- The divmod Unpack

divmod() returns a tuple of two values. Predict what happens when it is used in each of these three patterns.

```python
# Puzzle 8.1: divmod Unpacking Patterns

# Pattern A: store as a tuple
result = divmod(23, 4)
print(result)

# Pattern B: unpack into two variables
q, r = divmod(23, 4)
print(f"Quotient: {q}  Remainder: {r}")
```

```
# Pattern C: use in a conditional directly
if divmod(23, 4)[1] == 0:
    print("Divisible")
else:
    print("Not divisible")
```

Questions: What does Pattern A print? What is the type of result? In Pattern C, what does [1] do to the divmod return value, and which branch fires?

Puzzle 8.2 -- The bool() Edge Cases

bool() reveals Python's truthy/falsy rules. Some inputs produce surprising results. Predict every output before running.

```python
# Puzzle 8.2: bool() Edge Cases

print(bool(0.0))
print(bool(0.1))
print(bool("False"))
print(bool("0"))
print(bool([]))
print(bool([0]))
```

Questions: Why does bool("False") return True even though the word "False" suggests falsehood? Why does bool("0") return True when bool(0) returns False? What is the rule that determines whether a string is falsy?

Puzzle 8.3 -- sorted() Does Not Modify the Original

sorted() returns a new list and leaves the original unchanged. Predict all three outputs.

```python
# Puzzle 8.3: sorted() Immutability

raw_data = [30, 10, 50, 20, 40]
ordered  = sorted(raw_data)

print(raw_data)   # original
```

```
print(ordered)     # new sorted copy
print(raw_data is ordered)  # same object?
```

Questions: Are raw_data and ordered the same list or two different objects? What does the `is` operator check, and what does it return here? What built-in function could you call to confirm they are stored at different memory addresses?

Puzzle 8.4 -- isinstance() With a Tuple of Types

isinstance() accepts a single type or a tuple of types as its second argument. It returns True if the value matches any type in the tuple. Predict all four outputs.

```python
# Puzzle 8.4: isinstance() with Multiple Types

values = [42, 3.14, "hi", True]

for v in values:
    is_numeric = isinstance(v, (int, float))
    print(f"{v!r:8} -- numeric: {is_numeric}")
```

Questions: Does True pass the numeric check and why? In Python, bool is a subclass of int. How does that affect the isinstance() result for True? What would you add to the tuple to also accept strings?

Pillar 3 -- Code Audit: PEP 8 and Built-in Standards

The script below performs a basic data summary but contains six violations: non-descriptive variable names, missing whitespace around operators, manual reimplementation of built-in functions, no docstring, a magic number constant, and trailing logic that belongs inside a function. Identify every violation, record each in the audit table, and rewrite to production standards.

PILLAR 3 Code Audit -- PEP 8 and Built-in Standards

Instructions: Identify every violation. Record each in the table with the specific rule it breaks. Then rewrite the complete script to production standards.

Non-Compliant Script

```python
d=[90,78,85,92,70]
t=0
for x in d:
    t=t+x
avg=t/5
print("avg:",avg)
print("max:",max(d))
print("min:",min(d))
```

#	Violation Found	Rule Broken	Corrected Pattern
1	d, t, x, avg -- single-letter and non-descriptive names	PEP 8 naming: use descriptive lowercase_snake_case	scores, total, score, average
2	t=0, t=t+x, avg=t/5 -- no spaces around operators	E225: missing whitespace around operators	t = 0 | total += score | average = total / count
3	Manual loop to sum: for x in d: t=t+x	Built-in: sum() already exists. Never reimplement built-ins.	total = sum(scores)
4	Hardcoded /5 -- magic number tied to list length	Clarity: use len() instead of hardcoding the count	average = total / len(scores)
5	No enclosing function and no docstring	Design: wrap reusable logic in a function with a docstring	def summarise(scores): """..."""
6	print("avg:", avg) -- no f-string, weak label	Style: use f-strings for formatted output with descriptive labels	print(f"Average: {average:.1f}")

Production-Quality Refactored Script

```python
# ---------------------------------------------------
# Module  : score_summary.py
# Purpose : Summarises a list of student scores.
# Author  : Ayman Alzaid
# ---------------------------------------------------

def summarise(scores):
    """Print average, max, and min of a list of scores."""
    total   = sum(scores)             # built-in replaces manual loop
    count   = len(scores)             # dynamic -- not hardcoded
    average = round(total / count, 1)
```

```
    print(f"Average: {average}")
    print(f"Highest: {max(scores)}")
    print(f"Lowest:  {min(scores)}")

student_scores = [90, 78, 85, 92, 70]
summarise(student_scores)
```

Coding Challenge: Inventory Analyser

Chapter 8 Coding Challenge

Objective: Build a fully PEP 8 compliant inventory analysis module that uses at least eight built-in functions. Every requirement below must be satisfied.

>> Open with a PEP 8 header comment block and a module-level docstring.

>> Define prices as a list of at least six float values representing product prices.

>> Write a function analyse(prices) with a PEP 257 docstring that uses sum(), len(), round(), min(), max(), sorted(), and abs() to compute: total, count, average, cheapest, most expensive, price range (max - min), and a sorted copy.

>> Within the same function, use isinstance() to verify that every element in prices is a float or int before computing. If validation fails, return an error string.

>> Use enumerate() to print a ranked price list (1. cheapest, 2. second cheapest, etc.) using the sorted copy.

>> Use divmod() to show how many whole pounds and pence are in the total price.

>> Apply f-strings with :.2f formatting to all monetary output.

Chapter Summary

Concept	Key Takeaway
Built-in functions	Always available without import. Python provides 68; the 22 covered here handle the majority of everyday programming tasks.
int() / float() / str() / bool()	Type conversion. int() truncates floats. bool() is False for 0, empty strings, empty lists, and None.
abs() / round() / pow()	Numeric utilities. round(x, n) rounds to n decimal places using banker's rounding.
min() / max() / sum()	Aggregation. All three accept a sequence or multiple arguments. sum() requires an iterable.
divmod(a, b)	Returns (quotient, remainder) as a tuple. Equivalent to (a//b, a%b) in one call.
type() / isinstance()	Introspection. Use isinstance() for validation; it respects subclasses. Use type() for exact matching.
len()	Returns the number of elements in any sequence. Use len() instead of hardcoding counts.
sorted()	Returns a new sorted list. The original is unchanged. Pass reverse=True for descending order.
enumerate()	Adds index numbers to iteration. enumerate(items, start=1) starts counting from 1.
zip()	Pairs elements from two or more sequences. Stops at the shortest sequence.
PEP 8	The official Python style guide. Naming, whitespace, line length, imports, comments. Enforced automatically in professional environments.
Never reimplement built-ins	If sum(), min(), max(), or len() already does the job, use it. Manual loops for aggregation are a code smell.

CHAPTER 9

Loops and Iteration

Learning Objectives

1. Explain what a loop is, why iteration exists, and what problem repetition solves in software design.
2. Write a correctly structured while loop with an explicit condition and identify the three components that prevent infinite loops.
3. Write a for loop that iterates over a range, a string, and a list using correct syntax and indentation.
4. Use the range() function with one, two, and three arguments to generate specific integer sequences.
5. Apply break to exit a loop early when a target condition is met.
6. Apply continue to skip the current iteration and resume from the next.
7. Use the loop else clause to detect whether a loop completed without a break.
8. Write nested loops and trace the full execution sequence of the inner and outer iterations.
9. Identify and correct common loop errors: infinite loops, off-by-one errors, and misplaced break/continue.

Theoretical Foundation

The Problem Loops Solve

Every program examined so far executes each statement exactly once. That model collapses the moment a task must be repeated. Printing the numbers from 1 to 100 with sequential statements requires 100 lines of code. Processing every item in a customer order list of unknown length requires a different mechanism entirely. Copying and pasting code is not a solution. It is a symptom of missing the right tool.

A **loop** is the tool. It is a control structure that executes a block of code *repeatedly* until a condition stops being true. The block runs once, then again, then again, until the loop's exit condition is satisfied. A loop that processes 1000 items takes the same number of source lines as a loop that processes 1. The program scales. The code does not.

Two Types of Loop: while and for

Python provides two loop structures. They share the same indented-block syntax from Chapter 5 but differ in when they are appropriate.

A **while loop** repeats as long as a Boolean condition remains True. It is the right choice when the number of repetitions is not known in advance: keep asking the user for valid input until they provide it, keep running a simulation until a convergence threshold is reached, keep reading data until a sentinel value appears. The condition is re-evaluated before every iteration.

A **for loop** iterates over a sequence, visiting each item exactly once. It is the right choice when the collection of items to process is known: process each score in a grade list, step through each character in a string, execute a block exactly N times using `range()`. The loop ends automatically when the sequence is exhausted.

Figure 9.1 -- while vs for: Execution Model Comparison

Both loops repeat a block. The difference is in how they decide when to stop.

while loop		for loop
1. Evaluate condition if True >> run body if False >> exit 2. Run body block 3. Go back to step 1 4. Repeat until False	vs	**1. Get next item** from the sequence 2. Assign to variable 3. Run body block 4. Repeat for all items 5. Exit when done
Use when: count unknown		*Use when: count known / iterating*

The Three Components of a Safe while Loop

Every `while` loop that is not intentionally infinite must have three elements. Missing any one of them produces an **infinite loop** — a program that runs forever.

Component	What It Does	Example	What Happens If Missing
Initialisation	Sets the variable the condition checks before the loop starts	count = 0	NameError: the condition references an undefined variable
Condition	Evaluated before each iteration; loop continues while True	while count < 10:	SyntaxError: while with no condition
Update	Changes the variable inside the loop body so the condition eventually becomes False	count += 1	Infinite loop: condition never changes, loop runs forever

The range() Function: The for Loop's Counter

The `range()` function generates a sequence of integers on demand. It is almost always the argument to a `for` loop when the goal is to execute a block a specific number of times, rather than to process items from an existing collection. It accepts one, two, or three arguments.

Signature	Generates	Example	Output Sequence
range(stop)	Integers from 0 up to (not including) stop	range(5)	0, 1, 2, 3, 4
range(start, stop)	Integers from start up to (not including) stop	range(2, 7)	2, 3, 4, 5, 6
range(start, stop, step)	Integers from start, stepping by step, up to stop	range(0, 10, 2)	0, 2, 4, 6, 8
range(start, stop, -step)	Counts DOWN from start to stop + 1	range(10, 0, -2)	10, 8, 6, 4, 2

range() is Exclusive of the Stop Value

Rule: `range(n)` generates 0 through n-1. It never includes n itself.

Common mistake: Writing `range(1, 10)` to get 1 through 10. This produces 1 through 9 only. Use `range(1, 11)` for 1 through 10.

Memory note: range() does not create a list in memory. It generates each value on demand. This makes it efficient even for range(1000000).

Loop Control: break, continue, and pass

Three keywords modify how a loop executes from inside its body. They change the default behavior of running every iteration to completion.

Keyword	Effect	When to Use	What Continues After
break	Immediately exits the entire loop	A target condition is met mid-iteration (found a result, detected an error)	The first statement after the loop block
continue	Skips the rest of the current iteration and moves to the next	The current item should be ignored (e.g. filter out invalid values)	The next iteration of the same loop
pass	Does nothing — a no-op placeholder	When syntax requires a block but no action is needed yet	The next statement in the current iteration

The Loop else Clause

Python's loops have an optional `else` clause that most languages do not provide. The `else` block executes when the loop finishes normally — that is, when the while condition becomes False or the for sequence is exhausted *without* a `break` having been triggered. If `break` fires at any point, the `else` block is skipped entirely.

This is most useful for search loops. If you loop through a list looking for an item and use `break` when you find it, the `else` clause runs only when the item was *not* found. This eliminates the need for a separate Boolean flag variable to track whether the search succeeded.

Nested Loops

A **nested loop** is a loop placed inside the body of another loop. The inner loop runs to full completion for every single iteration of the outer loop. If the outer loop runs 3 times and the inner loop runs 4 times per outer iteration, the inner loop's body executes 12 times in total.

Nested loops are essential for working with grids, tables, coordinate systems, and any structure that has two dimensions. The outer loop handles rows; the inner loop handles columns, or vice versa. The variables in the two loops must have different names.

Formal Syntax and Declaration

while Loop Syntax

```python
# while loop -- Formal Syntax

# Initialise the variable BEFORE the loop
counter = 0

while counter < 5:        # condition re-checked before each iteration
    print(f"Iteration {counter}")  # body block
    counter += 1              # UPDATE: must change the condition variable

# Optional else: runs only if the while condition became False naturally
while counter < 3:
    counter += 1
else:
    print("Loop finished normally.")
```

for Loop Syntax

```python
# for loop -- Formal Syntax

# Pattern 1: iterate over a range
for i in range(5):
    print(i)  # prints 0 1 2 3 4

# Pattern 2: iterate over a list
scores = [88, 72, 95]
for score in scores:
    print(score)

# Pattern 3: iterate over a string character by character
for char in "Python":
    print(char)  # prints each letter on a new line
```

break, continue, and loop else

```python
# break -- exit loop immediately
for n in range(10):
    if n == 5:
        break             # exits when n reaches 5
    print(n)           # prints 0 1 2 3 4

# continue -- skip this iteration only
for n in range(6):
    if n % 2 == 0:
        continue          # skip even numbers
    print(n)           # prints 1 3 5

# else -- runs only if no break occurred
for n in range(5):
    if n == 9:  # never True
```

```
        break
else:
    print("No break occurred.")
```

Implementation and Code Examples

Example 1 -- while Loop: Input Validation Gate

The classic use of `while`: keep asking the user for valid input until they provide it. The number of attempts is unknown in advance, which makes `while` the correct choice over `for`. The loop exits naturally when a valid value is entered.

```python
# Example 1: Input Validation with while

age = -1  # initialise to a value that fails the condition

while age < 0 or age > 120:
    age = int(input("Enter your age (0-120): "))
    if age < 0 or age > 120:
        print("Invalid. Please enter a value between 0 and 120.")

print(f"Valid age entered: {age}")
```

Expected Output

```
Enter your age (0-120): -5
Invalid. Please enter a value between 0 and 120.
Enter your age (0-120): 200
Invalid. Please enter a value between 0 and 120.
Enter your age (0-120): 28
Valid age entered: 28
```

Example 2 -- for Loop with range(): Countdown Timer

Three-argument `range()` with a negative step generates a descending sequence. This example counts down from 5 to 1, then prints the launch message. Note that `range(5, 0, -1)` generates 5, 4, 3, 2, 1 — the stop value 0 is excluded, so 1 is the last number produced.

```python
# Example 2: for loop with range() -- Countdown

for seconds in range(5, 0, -1):
    print(f"T-minus {seconds}...")

print("Liftoff!")
```

Expected Output

```
T-minus 5...
T-minus 4...
T-minus 3...
T-minus 2...
T-minus 1...
Liftoff!
```

Example 3 -- break and continue: Score Filter

This example processes a list of scores. `continue` skips scores below 50 (invalid entries). `break` exits the loop when a perfect score of 100 is found, short-circuiting the rest of the list.

```python
# Example 3: break and continue in a for loop

scores = [72, 45, 88, 100, 91]

for score in scores:
    if score < 50:
        print(f"Skipping invalid score: {score}")
        continue              # go to next score
    if score == 100:
```

```
        print("Perfect score found! Stopping.")
        break                   # exit loop immediately
    print(f"Processing score: {score}")
```

Expected Output

```
Processing score: 72
Skipping invalid score: 45
Processing score: 88
Perfect score found! Stopping.
```

Example 4 -- Loop else: Linear Search

The `else` clause on a `for` loop is the cleanest way to implement a search that needs to report failure. The `else` block runs if and only if no `break` was executed. No flag variable needed.

```python
# Example 4: Loop else for Search

def find_prime(candidates):
    """Search a list for the first prime number."""
    for n in candidates:
        if n > 1 and all(n % i != 0 for i in range(2, n)):
            print(f"First prime found: {n}")
            break             # stop at first prime
    else:                   # runs ONLY if no break occurred
        print("No prime found in list.")

find_prime([4, 6, 9, 15])
find_prime([4, 6, 7, 10])
```

Expected Output

```
No prime found in list.
First prime found: 7
```

Example 5 -- Nested Loops: Multiplication Table

This example uses nested loops to generate a formatted multiplication table. The outer loop controls the row (multiplier 1 to 5). The inner loop controls the column (multiplier 1 to 5). The inner loop runs completely for every single iteration of the outer loop.

```python
# Example 5: Nested Loops -- Multiplication Table

# Header row
print("    ", end="")
for col in range(1, 6):
    print(f"{col:4}", end="")
print()
print("-" * 24)

# Nested loops for the table body
for row in range(1, 6):          # outer: rows 1-5
    print(f"{row:3}", end="")
    for col in range(1, 6):      # inner: cols 1-5
        print(f"{row * col:4}", end="")
    print()  # newline after each row
```

Expected Output

```
       1   2   3   4   5
------------------------
  1    1   2   3   4   5
  2    2   4   6   8  10
  3    3   6   9  12  15
  4    4   8  12  16  20
  5    5  10  15  20  25
```

The Active Learning Framework

Pillar 1 traces a while loop through its full iteration cycle, recording every variable change. Pillar 2 presents four puzzles: an off-by-one range error, an infinite loop detection, the break vs continue distinction, and nested loop execution counting. Pillar 3 audits a broken loop with five violations.

> **Active Learning Pillars: P1** Trace the interpreter line by line. **P2** Predict the output before running. **P3** Audit and refactor to PEP 8 standards. Verify every prediction at the terminal.

Pillar 1 -- Logic Exercise: while Loop Trace

Tracing a loop requires recording the state of every variable *before the condition is checked* on each iteration, then recording the state *after the body executes*. The trace ends the first time the condition evaluates to False.

Trace Rule 1: Record variable values at the start of each iteration, before the condition check. **Trace Rule 2:** Evaluate the condition using those values. If False, the loop ends here. **Trace Rule 3:** If True, execute the body and record the updated values. **Trace Rule 4:** Return to Rule 1 for the next iteration.

PILLAR 1 Logic Exercise

Instructions: Trace the while loop below through every iteration. Complete the Iteration Trace Table. Record exact variable values after each body execution. Do not run the code.

Python

```python
# Pillar 1: while Loop Trace

x = 1
total = 0

while x <= 5:
    if x % 2 == 0:
        total += x          # add only even numbers
    x += 1

print(f"Sum of evens: {total}")
```

Iteration Trace Table

Iteration	x (before check)	Condition x <= 5	x % 2 == 0?	total after body	x after body
1	1	True	?	?	2
2	2	True	?	?	3
3	3	True	?	?	4
4	4	True	?	?	5
5	5	True	?	?	6
6	6	False -- loop ends	--	--	--

Challenge Questions: What does print output? Which iterations add to total and which do not? If the condition were x < 5 instead of x <= 5, which iterations would be removed from the trace?

Pillar 2 -- Mysterious Output Puzzles: Predict Before You Run

Four puzzles test the most common loop mistakes. Predict the exact console output before running any code.

PILLAR 2 Mysterious Output Puzzles

Instructions: Predict the complete output for each puzzle. Record all predictions first. Then execute and compare.

Puzzle 9.1 -- The Off-by-One range

Predict the exact output of all three print statements. Count every value each range produces.

```python
# Puzzle 9.1: range() boundaries

print(list(range(5)))
print(list(range(1, 5)))
print(list(range(1, 10, 3)))
```

Questions: How many values does each range produce? Which of the three includes its start value? Which includes its stop value? What would you write to produce the list [10, 9, 8, 7, 6]?

Puzzle 9.2 -- The Infinite Loop Detector

One of these three while loops is infinite. Identify which one and explain exactly why it never terminates.

```
• • • Python

# Puzzle 9.2: Which loop never ends?

# Loop A
n = 10
while n > 0:
    n -= 3

# Loop B
n = 1
while n != 10:
    n += 2

# Loop C
n = 0
while n < 100:
    n *= 2
```

Questions: Which loop is infinite and why can the condition never become False? What does Loop A ultimately print? What is the final value of n in Loop A?

Puzzle 9.3 -- break vs continue

Two loops look nearly identical. One uses break, the other uses continue. Predict both outputs in full.

```
• • • Python

# Puzzle 9.3: break vs continue

# Script A: using break
for i in range(1, 6):
    if i == 3:
        break
    print(i)

# Script B: using continue
for i in range(1, 6):
    if i == 3:
```

```
        continue
    print(i)
```

Questions: How many lines does each script print? How does the output differ? In Script B, does i == 3 ever get printed? Where does execution go after continue fires?

Puzzle 9.4 -- Nested Loop Execution Count

Predict the exact output and count how many times the innermost print statement executes.

```python
# Puzzle 9.4: Nested Loop Execution Count

count = 0
for outer in range(1, 4):  # outer: 1 2 3
    for inner in range(1, outer + 1):  # inner runs 1..outer times
        count += 1
        print(f"outer={outer} inner={inner}")

print(f"Total executions: {count}")
```

Questions: How many lines does the inner print produce? Why does the inner range change on each outer iteration? What is the value of count when the loops finish?

Pillar 3 -- Code Audit: Loop Violations

The script below attempts to compute a running total of valid positive numbers. It contains five violations: a missing initialisation variable, an infinite loop risk, a misindented update statement, a break used where continue is needed, and non-descriptive variable names. Identify each violation, record it in the audit table, and rewrite to production standards.

PILLAR 3 Code Audit -- Loop Violations

Instructions: Identify every violation. Record each in the table. Rewrite the complete script to production standards.

Non-Compliant Script

```python
# Collect positive numbers until user enters 0, print running total

while True:
    x = int(input("Enter number: "))
    if x < 0:
        break              # BUG: should skip, not stop
    if x == 0:
        break
t = t + x          # BUG: t not initialised; also misindented
print("total:",t)
```

#	Violation Found	Rule Broken	Corrected Pattern
1	t is never initialised before the loop -- NameError on first iteration	Initialisation: always declare and set the accumulator before the loop	total = 0 (before the while)
2	Variable names x and t are single-letter and non-descriptive	Naming: use descriptive snake_case names	user_input, running_total
3	break on negative input stops the whole loop instead of skipping	Logic: negative numbers should be ignored, not end the session -- use continue	if user_input < 0: continue
4	total update line t = t + x is misindented -- outside the loop body	Indentation: the accumulator update must be inside the loop (4 spaces in)	running_total += user_input (indented inside while)
5	print("total:",t) uses old-style comma print instead of f-string	Style: use f-strings for formatted output	print(f"Running total: {running_total}")

Production-Quality Refactored Script

```python
# --------------------------------------------------
# Module   : running_total.py
# Purpose  : Collects positive numbers, skips negatives,
#            stops on 0, prints the running total.
# Author   : Ayman Alzaid
# --------------------------------------------------

running_total = 0  # initialise BEFORE the loop
```

```
while True:
    user_input = int(input("Enter a positive number (0 to stop): "))

    if user_input == 0:
        break                    # exit cleanly on sentinel value

    if user_input < 0:
        print("Negative numbers are skipped.")
        continue                 # skip, do not add to total

    running_total += user_input       # properly indented inside loop
    print(f"Running total: {running_total}")

print(f"Final total: {running_total}")
```

Coding Challenge: Number Guessing Game

Chapter 9 Coding Challenge

Objective: Build a complete number guessing game using loops, conditionals, and functions. Every requirement below must be satisfied.

>> Open with a PEP 8 compliant header comment block.

>> Write a function play_round(secret, max_attempts) that uses a while loop to give the player up to max_attempts guesses.

>> Inside the loop: collect an integer guess, print "Too high", "Too low", or "Correct!" using an if-elif-else chain.

>> Use break when the player guesses correctly. Use the loop else clause to print "Out of attempts! The number was X." if they do not guess in time.

>> Track and display the number of attempts used at the end of a successful round.

>> Write a for loop in main code that plays 3 rounds with secrets [42, 17, 88] and max_attempts=5.

>> Add a continue in the outer for loop that skips any round where the secret is below 20 (to demonstrate continue).

Chapter Summary

Concept	Key Takeaway
while loop	Repeats while a condition is True. Requires initialisation, condition, and update. Missing the update causes an infinite loop.
for loop	Iterates over a sequence (range, list, string). Ends automatically when the sequence is exhausted.
range(stop)	Generates 0 to stop-1. The stop value is never included.
range(start, stop, step)	Full three-argument form. Use negative step to count down.
break	Immediately exits the entire loop and jumps to the first statement after it.
continue	Skips the rest of the current iteration and moves to the next one.
pass	No-op placeholder. Does nothing. Allows syntactically required blocks to remain empty.
Loop else	Executes only when the loop condition became False (while) or sequence exhausted (for) without a break firing.
Nested loops	Inner loop runs completely for each outer iteration. Total executions = outer_count x inner_count.
Infinite loop	A while loop where the condition never becomes False because the update is missing, wrong, or unreachable.
Off-by-one error	range(1, 10) produces 1 to 9, not 1 to 10. The stop value is always excluded.
Accumulator pattern	Initialise total = 0 before the loop. Add inside the loop. Print after the loop.

CHAPTER 10

Python Lists

Learning Objectives

1. Create a list using square-bracket literal syntax and the list() constructor.
2. Access individual elements using positive and negative indexing.
3. Extract sub-sequences using slicing with start, stop, and step arguments.
4. Explain mutability: why lists can be modified in place while strings cannot.
5. Apply the core list methods: append, extend, insert, remove, pop, sort, reverse, index, count, and copy.
6. Iterate over a list using a for loop and the enumerate() function.
7. Use list comprehensions to create filtered and transformed lists in one line.
8. Combine lists with functions to build modular, reusable data-processing pipelines.
9. Identify and avoid common list errors: index out of range, mutation during iteration, and shallow copy confusion.

Theoretical Foundation

What a List Is

Every variable introduced so far holds a single value: one integer, one string, one Boolean. Real programs deal with collections. A classroom has many students. An invoice has many line items. A sensor produces many readings. A Python **list** is the primary tool for holding multiple values in a single, ordered, named container.

A list stores its elements in a fixed sequence. The order is preserved. Element 0 is always element 0 unless the list is explicitly rearranged. A list can hold values of different types in the same container: a string, an integer, a Boolean, and a float can all live in the same list simultaneously. Lists are also **mutable** — their contents can be changed after creation, unlike strings, which are immutable.

Indexing: Accessing Individual Elements

Every element in a list has a position called its **index**. Indices start at `0` for the first element, not at 1. A list of 5 elements has valid indices 0, 1, 2, 3, and 4. Attempting to access index 5 raises an `IndexError`.

Python also supports **negative indexing**. `-1` always refers to the last element, `-2` to the second-to-last, and so on. Negative indices count backward from the end of the list. For a list of length n, the valid negative index range is -n through -1.

Figure 10.1 -- List Structure: Positive and Negative Indices

The list below holds five elements of mixed types. Blue labels above each cell show the positive index. Red labels below show the negative index. Both refer to the same element.

students[0] through students[4] -- a list of 5 mixed-type elements				
[0]	[1]	[2]	[3]	[4]
"Fatima"	88	"B+"	True	95.5
[-5]	[-4]	[-3]	[-2]	[-1]
str	*int*	*str*	*bool*	*float*

Blue = positive index | Red = negative index | Lists are ordered, mutable, and accept mixed types

Slicing: Extracting Sub-Lists

A **slice** extracts a portion of a list and returns it as a new list. The original list is not modified. Slice syntax uses square brackets with a colon: `list[start:stop]`. The result includes elements from `start` up to but not including `stop`. A third argument adds a step: `list[start:stop:step]`.

Slice Expression	Meaning	Example on [0,1,2,3,4]	Result
lst[1:4]	Elements at index 1, 2, 3	[0,1,2,3,4][1:4]	[1, 2, 3]
lst[:3]	From start to index 2	[0,1,2,3,4][:3]	[0, 1, 2]
lst[2:]	From index 2 to end	[0,1,2,3,4][2:]	[2, 3, 4]
lst[:]	Full copy of the list	[0,1,2,3,4][:]	[0, 1, 2, 3, 4]
lst[::2]	Every second element	[0,1,2,3,4][::2]	[0, 2, 4]
lst[::-1]	Reversed list	[0,1,2,3,4][::-1]	[4, 3, 2, 1, 0]

Mutability: Lists Can Be Changed In Place

A string is immutable — you cannot change one character without creating a new string object. A list is **mutable** — you can change, add, or remove elements directly. Assigning to an index modifies the list at that position: `my_list[2] = "new value"` replaces element 2 without creating a new list.

Mutability changes how assignment works. Writing `b = a` where `a` is a list does *not* create a copy. It creates a second name pointing at the same list. Changing `b` changes `a` as well. To create a true independent copy, use `a.copy()`, `a[:]`, or `list(a)`.

The Assignment vs Copy Trap
Wrong: `b = a` -- both names point to the same list. Mutating b changes a.
Correct: `b = a.copy()` or `b = a[:]` -- b is a new, independent list.
Check: Use `a is b` to test identity (same object). Use `a == b` to test equality (same contents).

Core List Methods

A list method is a function attached to a list object. It is called using dot notation: `my_list.method_name(arguments)`. Some methods modify the list in place and return `None`. Others return a new value without modifying the list.

Method	Signature	Effect / Returns	Example
append()	lst.append(x)	Adds x to the end. Returns None.	scores.append(95)
extend()	lst.extend(iterable)	Adds all items from iterable to end. Returns None.	scores.extend([88, 72])
insert()	lst.insert(i, x)	Inserts x before index i. Returns None.	names.insert(0, "Fatima")
remove()	lst.remove(x)	Removes first occurrence of x. Raises ValueError if absent.	scores.remove(72)
pop()	lst.pop(i=-1)	Removes and returns element at index i. Default: last item.	last = scores.pop()
sort()	lst.sort(reverse=False)	Sorts list in place. Returns None.	scores.sort()
reverse()	lst.reverse()	Reverses list in place. Returns None.	scores.reverse()
index()	lst.index(x)	Returns index of first occurrence of x. Raises ValueError if absent.	pos = names.index("Hadi")
count()	lst.count(x)	Returns number of times x appears in the list.	n = scores.count(88)
copy()	lst.copy()	Returns a shallow copy of the list.	backup = scores.copy()
clear()	lst.clear()	Removes all elements. Returns None.	scores.clear()

List Comprehensions

A **list comprehension** is a compact syntax for creating a new list by applying an expression to each item in an existing sequence. It replaces a three-line for-loop-and-append pattern with a single readable line.

```python
# Traditional for loop approach
squares = []
for n in range(1, 6):
    squares.append(n ** 2)

# Equivalent list comprehension -- one line
squares = [n ** 2 for n in range(1, 6)]

# With a filter condition -- only even squares
even_squares = [n ** 2 for n in range(1, 11) if n % 2 == 0]

print(squares)       # [1, 4, 9, 16, 25]
print(even_squares)  # [4, 16, 36, 64, 100]
```

Formal Syntax and Declaration

Creating Lists

```python
# List Creation Syntax

# Literal syntax -- most common
empty    = []
numbers  = [1, 2, 3, 4, 5]
names    = ["Fatima", "Hadi", "Ellie"]
mixed    = ["Fatima", 88, "B+", True]

# From range -- useful for numeric sequences
one_to_ten = list(range(1, 11))

# Indexing and slicing
print(names[0])       # "Fatima"  -- first element
print(names[-1])      # "Ellie" -- last element
print(numbers[1:4])     # [2, 3, 4]
print(numbers[::-1])    # [5, 4, 3, 2, 1]
```

List Comprehension Syntax

```
Python
# List Comprehension -- Formal Syntax

# [expression  for  variable  in  iterable]
doubled = [x * 2 for x in range(5)]

# [expression  for  variable  in  iterable  if  condition]
positives = [x for x in [-3,1,-2,4,5] if x > 0]

print(doubled)    # [0, 2, 4, 6, 8]
print(positives)  # [1, 4, 5]
```

Implementation and Code Examples

Example 1 -- Building and Modifying a List

This example demonstrates the core mutation methods: `append()`, `insert()`, `remove()`, and `pop()`. Each method modifies the list in place. Printing the list after each operation shows the cumulative effect.

```
Python
# Example 1: Building and Modifying a List

cart = ["bread", "milk", "eggs"]
print(f"Initial:  {cart}")

cart.append("butter")          # add to end
print(f"Append:   {cart}")

cart.insert(1, "cheese")       # insert at index 1
print(f"Insert:   {cart}")

cart.remove("milk")           # remove first "milk"
```

```
print(f"Remove:   {cart}")

last_item = cart.pop()          # remove and return last item
print(f"Popped:   {last_item}  |  Cart: {cart}")
```

Expected Output

```
Initial:  ['bread', 'milk', 'eggs']
Append:   ['bread', 'milk', 'eggs', 'butter']
Insert:   ['bread', 'cheese', 'milk', 'eggs', 'butter']
Remove:   ['bread', 'cheese', 'eggs', 'butter']
Popped:   butter  |  Cart: ['bread', 'cheese', 'eggs']
```

Example 2 -- Sorting and Searching

This example contrasts `sort()` (modifies in place, returns `None`) with `sorted()` (returns a new list, original unchanged). It also demonstrates `index()` for searching and `count()` for frequency.

```python
# Example 2: Sorting and Searching

scores = [72, 88, 95, 65, 88, 77]

# sorted() -- returns new list, original unchanged
ordered = sorted(scores)
print(f"Original: {scores}")
print(f"Sorted:   {ordered}")

# sort() -- modifies in place
scores.sort(reverse=True)
print(f"In-place descending: {scores}")

# index() and count()
print(f"First 88 at index: {scores.index(88)}")
print(f"Count of 88: {scores.count(88)}")
```

Expected Output
`Original: [72, 88, 95, 65, 88, 77]`
`Sorted:   [65, 72, 77, 88, 88, 95]`
`In-place descending: [95, 88, 88, 77, 72, 65]`
`First 88 at index: 1`
`Count of 88: 2`

Example 3 -- Iterating with for and enumerate()

When you need only the value from each element, use a plain `for` loop. When you also need the position, use `enumerate()` to get both index and value together. This avoids the error-prone `range(len(list))` pattern.

```python
# Example 3: Iterating with for and enumerate()

students = ["Fatima", "Hadi", "Ellie"]
grades   = [88, 72, 95]

# Plain for -- value only
for student in students:
    print(f"Student: {student}")

# enumerate() -- index and value together
print("---")
for rank, name in enumerate(students, start=1):
    grade = grades[rank - 1]
    print(f"{rank}. {name:<10} {grade}")
```

Expected Output
`Student: Fatima`
`Student: Hadi`
`Student: Ellie`
`---`
`1. Fatima     88`
`2. Hadi       72`

```
3. Ellie    95
```

Example 4 -- List Comprehensions in Practice

Three practical list comprehension patterns: transformation (apply an operation to every element), filtering (keep only elements that pass a condition), and combined transformation with filtering.

```python
# Example 4: List Comprehension Patterns

raw_scores = [45, 82, 91, 38, 76, 55]

# Pattern 1: Transformation -- scale all scores by +5 bonus
bonus_scores  = [s + 5 for s in raw_scores]
print(f"Bonus:     {bonus_scores}")

# Pattern 2: Filtering -- keep only passing scores (>= 50)
passing       = [s for s in raw_scores if s >= 50]
print(f"Passing:   {passing}")

# Pattern 3: Transform + filter -- grades for scores >= 50
def to_grade(s): return "A" if s >= 90 else "B" if s >= 75 else "C"
letter_grades = [to_grade(s) for s in raw_scores if s >= 50]
print(f"Grades:    {letter_grades}")
```

Expected Output

```
Bonus:     [50, 87, 96, 43, 81, 60]
Passing:   [82, 91, 76, 55]
Grades:    ['B', 'A', 'B', 'C']
```

Example 5 -- Complete Program: Student Report Builder

This example builds a complete report system using three cooperating functions, all built around lists. It brings together list creation, methods, built-in functions, list comprehensions, and loop iteration in a fully PEP 8 compliant module.

```python
# ---------------------------------------------------
# Module  : student_report.py
# Purpose : Processes student scores using lists.
# Author  : Ayman Alzaid
# ---------------------------------------------------

def get_statistics(scores):
    """Return a dict of statistics for a score list."""
    return {
        "count"  : len(scores),
        "average": round(sum(scores) / len(scores), 1),
        "highest": max(scores),
        "lowest" : min(scores),
        "passing": len([s for s in scores if s >= 50])
    }

def print_report(names, scores):
    """Print a formatted report for all students."""
    stats = get_statistics(scores)
    print(f"Students: {stats['count']}  Avg: {stats['average']}  Pass rate: 
{stats['passing']}/{stats['count']}")
    print("-" * 32)
    for i, name in enumerate(names):
        status = "Pass" if scores[i] >= 50 else "Fail"
        print(f"{name:<12} {scores[i]:>5}  {status}")

student_names  = ["Fatima", "Hadi", "Ellie", "Diana"]
student_scores = [88, 45, 91, 67]
print_report(student_names, student_scores)
```

Expected Output

```
Students: 4  Avg: 72.8  Pass rate: 3/4
--------------------------------
Fatima          88  Pass
Hadi            45  Fail
Ellie        91  Pass
Diana          67  Pass
```

The Active Learning Framework

Pillar 1 traces a script that builds, mutates, and iterates a list through a full state trace. Pillar 2 presents four puzzles: the alias trap, sort() returning None, slice boundaries, and list comprehension filtering. Pillar 3 audits a broken grade processor with five violations.

> **Active Learning Pillars:** **P1** Trace the interpreter line by line. **P2** Predict the output before running. **P3** Audit and refactor to PEP 8 standards. Verify every prediction at the terminal.

Pillar 1 -- Logic Exercise: List State Trace

Tracing list operations requires recording the complete state of the list after every mutation. Methods like `append()`, `sort()`, and `pop()` change the list in place. The list is the same object in memory throughout — only its contents change.

PILLAR 1 Logic Exercise

Instructions: Trace the script below one statement at a time. After each operation that modifies the list, record its complete new state. Record the value of any variable assigned from a list operation. Do not run the code.

Python

```python
# Pillar 1: List State Trace

data = [5, 3, 8, 1, 9, 3]
data.append(7)
data.remove(3)          # removes FIRST 3 only
data.sort()
x = data.pop(0)         # remove and return index 0
data.insert(2, 10)
total = sum(data)
print(data, x, total)
```

List State Trace Table

Statement	data after operation	Other variables
data = [5,3,8,1,9,3]	[5, 3, 8, 1, 9, 3]	--
data.append(7)	? fill in	--
data.remove(3)	? fill in (first 3 removed)	--
data.sort()	? fill in	--
x = data.pop(0)	? fill in	x = ? fill in
data.insert(2, 10)	? fill in	--
total = sum(data)	unchanged	total = ? fill in
print(data, x, total)	--	Output = ? fill in

Challenge Questions: Why does remove(3) only remove one 3 even though two exist? What does pop(0) return and what is the state of data immediately after? What does the final print line display?

Pillar 2 -- Mysterious Output Puzzles: Predict Before You Run

Four puzzles test the most common list mistakes. Predict all output before running.

PILLAR 2 Mysterious Output Puzzles

Instructions: Predict the complete output for each puzzle. Record all predictions first. Then execute and compare.

Puzzle 10.1 -- The Alias Trap

Predict all four print outputs and explain why changing b affects a.

```python
# Puzzle 10.1: Assignment creates an alias, not a copy

a = [1, 2, 3]
b = a                    # alias, not a copy
c = a.copy()              # true independent copy

b.append(4)
c.append(99)

print(a)
```

```
print(b)
print(c)
print(a is b, a is c)
```

Questions: What does each print output? Why does appending to b change a but appending to c does not? What does the `is` operator check and what does the last line print?

Puzzle 10.2 -- The sort() Returns None Trap

A beginner tries to sort and store the result in one line. Predict the output and explain why it fails.

```python
# Puzzle 10.2: sort() returns None

numbers = [3, 1, 4, 1, 5]

# Attempt to sort AND store in one line
sorted_nums = numbers.sort()
print(sorted_nums)
print(numbers)
```

Questions: What does `sorted_nums` contain and why? What state is `numbers` in after the call? What are the two correct ways to sort and store the result?

Puzzle 10.3 -- Slice Boundary Logic

Predict all four outputs. Count every element each slice produces.

```python
# Puzzle 10.3: Slice Boundaries

lst = [10, 20, 30, 40, 50]

print(lst[1:-1])
print(lst[-3:])
print(lst[::-2])
print(lst[10:])  # index beyond list length
```

Questions: What does [1:-1] mean in plain English? What does [::-2] produce and why? Does [10:] raise an IndexError or return something else?

Puzzle 10.4 -- List Comprehension with Function Call

Predict both outputs. Trace what the comprehension produces step by step.

```python
# Puzzle 10.4: Comprehension with Function and Condition

words = ["python", "is", "fun", "and", "powerful"]

long_upper = [w.upper() for w in words if len(w) > 3]
lengths    = [len(w) for w in words]

print(long_upper)
print(lengths)
```

Questions: Which words are excluded by the `len(w) > 3` condition? What are the two printed lists in full? What does `.upper()` do to each word?

Pillar 3 -- Code Audit: List Handling Violations

The script below attempts to collect and process exam scores entered by the user. It contains five violations: mutating a list during iteration, storing the None return of sort(), using a raw index loop instead of enumerate(), non-descriptive names, and no docstring on the function. Identify each violation, record it, and rewrite to production standards.

PILLAR 3 Code Audit -- List Handling

Instructions: Identify every violation. Record each in the table. Rewrite the complete script to production standards.

Non-Compliant Script

```python
def proc(d):
    d2 = d.sort()           # BUG: sort() returns None
```

```
    for i in range(len(d)):   # BUG: use enumerate()
        print(i, d[i])

scores = [70, 85, 90]
for s in scores:          # BUG: mutating during iteration
    if s < 80:
        scores.remove(s)
proc(scores)
```

#	Violation Found	Rule Broken	Corrected Pattern
1	def proc(d) -- no docstring, non-descriptive name and parameter	PEP 257 + naming: functions need a docstring and descriptive names	def print_sorted_scores(scores): """..."""
2	d2 = d.sort() -- stores None	API rule: sort() modifies in place and returns None. Use sorted() to get a new sorted list.	sorted_scores = sorted(scores)
3	range(len(d)) with manual index access d[i]	Style: use enumerate() when you need both index and value	for i, score in enumerate(scores):
4	Mutating scores inside a for loop over scores	Safety rule: never add or remove elements from a list while iterating over it. Iterate over a copy.	for s in scores.copy(): ...
5	Variable names d, d2, s, i are non-descriptive	Naming: use descriptive snake_case names throughout	scores, sorted_scores, score, index

Production-Quality Refactored Script

```
Python
# --------------------------------------------------
# Module  : score_processor.py
# Purpose : Filters and displays a sorted score list.
# Author  : Ayman Alzaid
# --------------------------------------------------

def print_sorted_scores(scores):
    """Print scores with rank using sorted order."""
    for rank, score in enumerate(sorted(scores), start=1):
        print(f"{rank}. {score}")

raw_scores = [70, 85, 90]
```

```
# Iterate over a copy to avoid mutation-during-iteration bug
passing_scores = [s for s in raw_scores if s >= 80]

print_sorted_scores(passing_scores)
```

Coding Challenge: Playlist Manager

Chapter 10 Coding Challenge

Objective: Build a playlist management system that uses lists as its core data structure. Every requirement below must be satisfied.

- >> Open with a PEP 8 compliant header comment block and module-level docstring.
- >> Create a playlist as a list of song title strings. Start with at least four songs.
- >> Write add_song(playlist, title) that appends to the playlist and prints confirmation.
- >> Write remove_song(playlist, title) that removes the song if it exists (use a conditional to check first with "in" operator), or prints "Not found" if not.
- >> Write display_playlist(playlist) that uses enumerate(start=1) to print a numbered list.
- >> Write find_song(playlist, title) using a for loop with loop else: print position if found, "Not in playlist" via the else clause.
- >> Write a list comprehension that creates a new list of all song titles converted to uppercase.
- >> Use all five functions in a demonstration script that adds, removes, displays, and searches.

Chapter Summary

Concept	Key Takeaway
List creation	Square bracket literals or list() constructor. Lists are ordered, mutable, and accept mixed types.
Indexing	Starts at 0. Negative indices count from the end: -1 is last. IndexError if out of range.
Slicing	lst[start:stop:step]. Stop is excluded. lst[:] copies the list. lst[::-1] reverses it.
Mutability	Lists can be changed in place. Strings cannot. Assignment creates an alias, not a copy.
copy()	Use a.copy(), a[:], or list(a) to create an independent copy. a = b creates an alias.
append() vs extend()	append(x) adds x as one element. extend(iter) adds all items from iter individually.
sort() vs sorted()	sort() modifies in place, returns None. sorted() returns a new list, original unchanged.
pop()	Removes and returns the element. Default removes last. pop(0) removes first.
remove()	Removes the first occurrence only. Raises ValueError if not found.
enumerate()	Use for loops that need both index and value. Cleaner than range(len(lst)).
List comprehension	[expression for var in iterable if condition]. Replaces loop + append with one line.
Mutation during iteration	Never add or remove from a list while looping over it. Iterate over a copy instead.

CHAPTER 11

Strings as Sequences

Learning Objectives

1. Explain the relationship between strings and sequences, and identify how string indexing and slicing follow the same rules as lists.
2. Apply positive and negative indexing to access individual characters in a string.
3. Extract substrings using slicing with start, stop, and step arguments.
4. Explain string immutability and describe why assignment to a character index raises a TypeError.
5. Use string operators: + for concatenation, * for repetition, and in for membership testing.
6. Apply the six categories of string methods: case, testing, search, modify, split/join, and format.
7. Use escape sequences to embed special characters inside string literals.
8. Write advanced f-string expressions using alignment, width, and precision format specifiers.
9. Build a text analysis function that uses multiple string methods cooperatively.

Theoretical Foundation

Strings Are Sequences

Chapter 10 introduced the list as Python's primary ordered sequence. A string is also a sequence -- a sequence of characters. Every rule learned in Chapter 10 about indexing and slicing applies identically to strings. The first character is at index 0. The last is at index `-1`. `len()` returns the number of characters. Slicing extracts a substring. The `in` operator tests whether a character or substring is present.

The critical difference between strings and lists is **immutability**. A list element can be replaced: `my_list[0] = "new"` works. A string character cannot: `my_str[0] = "J"` raises a `TypeError` immediately. To "change" a string, you must create a new one. Every string method that appears to modify a string actually returns a brand new string object, leaving the original completely unchanged.

Figure 11.1 -- String Structure: Characters, Indices, and Immutability

The string below is a sequence of six character slots. Each slot has a positive index (blue) and a negative index (red).

word = "Python" -- a string of 6 characters					
[0]	[1]	[2]	[3]	[4]	[5]
"P"	"y"	"t"	"h"	"o"	"n"
[-6]	[-5]	[-4]	[-3]	[-2]	[-1]

```
len("Python") = 6   |   word[0] = "P"   |   word[-1] =
         "n"   |   word[2:5] = "tho"
```

Immutable: word[0] = "J" raises TypeError -- strings cannot be changed in place

String Operators

Three operators work directly on strings without requiring a method call.

Operator	Name	Example	Result	Notes
+	Concatenation	"Hello" + " " + "World"	"Hello World"	Both operands must be strings. str + int raises TypeError.
*	Repetition	"ha" * 3	"hahaha"	Repeats the string n times. n must be an integer.
in	Membership	"py" in "python"	True	Tests whether a substring appears anywhere in the string.
not in	Non-membership	"z" not in "python"	True	Inverse of in. Returns True if substring is absent.

Escape Sequences

An **escape sequence** is a two-character combination beginning with a backslash that represents a special character inside a string literal. Without escape sequences, it would be impossible to embed a newline, a tab, or a quotation mark inside a string.

Escape Sequence	Represents	Example	Output
\n	Newline (moves to next line)	print("Line 1\nLine 2")	Line 1 then Line 2 on separate lines
\t	Horizontal tab	print("Col1\tCol2")	Col1 followed by a tab stop then Col2
\\\\	Literal backslash	print("C:\\\\Users")	C:\\Users
\'	Single quote inside single-quoted string	print('It\'s fine')	It's fine
\"	Double quote inside double-quoted string	print("She said \"hi\"")	She said "hi"
\r	Carriage return	Rarely used directly	Moves cursor to start of current line

Multi-Line Strings

Triple quotes (`"""` or `'''`) allow a string to span multiple lines without explicit `\n` escape sequences. Every newline inside the triple-quoted block is included literally in the string. Triple-quoted strings are used for docstrings (Chapter 7), long paragraphs of text, and multi-line output templates.

String Methods: Six Categories

Python's string type provides over 40 built-in methods. They fall into six functional categories. Every method returns a new string or a value -- the original string is never modified.

Figure 11.2 -- String Method Categories at a Glance

Case	Testing	Search	Modify	Split/Join	Format
`upper()` `lower()` `title()` `capitalize()`	`isalpha()` `isdigit()` `startswith()` `endswith()`	`find()` `rfind()` `index()` `count()`	`replace()` `strip()` `lstrip()` `rstrip()`	`split()` `join()` `splitlines()`	`center()` `ljust()` `rjust()` `zfill()`

Category 1: Case Methods

Method	Returns	Example	Result
upper()	All uppercase	"hello".upper()	"HELLO"
lower()	All lowercase	"HELLO".lower()	"hello"
title()	First letter of each word capitalised	"hello world".title()	"Hello World"
capitalize()	First letter capitalised, rest lower	"hELLO".capitalize()	"Hello"
swapcase()	Upper becomes lower and vice versa	"Hello".swapcase()	"hELLO"

Category 2: Testing Methods (return Boolean)

Method	Returns True when...	Example
isalpha()	All characters are letters (no spaces, digits, or symbols)	"Python".isalpha() >> True
isdigit()	All characters are digits 0-9	"123".isdigit() >> True
isalnum()	All characters are letters or digits	"abc123".isalnum() >> True

Method	Returns True when...	Example
isspace()	All characters are whitespace (space, tab, newline)	" ".isspace() >> True
islower()	All cased characters are lowercase	"hello".islower() >> True
isupper()	All cased characters are uppercase	"HELLO".isupper() >> True
startswith(s)	String begins with substring s	"Python".startswith("Py") >> True
endswith(s)	String ends with substring s	"Python".endswith("on") >> True

Category 3: Search Methods

Method	Returns	Raises on miss?	Example
find(s)	Index of first occurrence of s, or -1 if absent	No -- returns -1	"python".find("th") >> 2
rfind(s)	Index of last occurrence of s, or -1	No -- returns -1	"abcabc".rfind("b") >> 4
index(s)	Index of first occurrence of s	Yes -- ValueError	"python".index("th") >> 2
count(s)	Number of non-overlapping occurrences	No -- returns 0	"hello".count("l") >> 2

find() vs index(): Which to Use

Use find() when the substring might not be present. It returns -1 safely, so you can check the result without a try/except.

Use index() when the substring must exist and its absence is an error condition you want to detect immediately.

Category 4: Modify Methods

Method	Returns	Example	Result
replace(old,new)	New string with all old replaced by new	"hello world".replace("world","Python")	"hello Python"
strip()	Copy with leading and trailing whitespace removed	" hello ".strip()	"hello"

Method	Returns	Example	Result
lstrip()	Copy with leading whitespace removed	" hello ".lstrip()	"hello "
rstrip()	Copy with trailing whitespace removed	" hello ".rstrip()	" hello"

Category 5: Split and Join

These two methods are inverses of each other. `split()` breaks a string into a list of substrings by a delimiter. `join()` merges a list of strings into one string using a separator. Together they form the foundation of all text parsing and formatting in Python.

Method	Returns	Example	Result
split(sep)	List of substrings split by sep. Default splits on whitespace.	"a,b,c".split(",")	["a","b","c"]
split()	Splits on any whitespace, removes empty strings.	"hi there".split()	["hi","there"]
join(lst)	"separator".join(list) -- merges list items with separator between each.	" ".join(["A","B","C"])	"A B C"
splitlines()	List of lines split at newline characters.	"L1\nL2\nL3".splitlines()	["L1","L2","L3"]

Advanced f-String Format Specifiers

Chapter 3 introduced f-strings for basic output. The `:.2f` specifier for decimal precision was covered there. f-strings support a full mini-language for controlling width, alignment, and padding.

Specifier	Meaning	Example	Output
:<10	Left-align, width 10	"f"{'hi':<10}|"	hi |
:>10	Right-align, width 10	f"{'hi':>10}|"	hi|
:^10	Centre-align, width 10	f"{'hi':^10}|"	hi |
:0>5	Right-align, pad with zeros	f"{7:0>5}"	00007
:.2f	Float, 2 decimal places	f"{3.14159:.2f}"	3.14
:,	Integer with comma thousands separator	f"{1000000:,}"	1,000,000
:>10.2f	Right-align float, width 10, 2 dp	f"{3.14:>10.2f}"	3.14

Formal Syntax and Declaration

String Creation and Common Patterns

```python
# String Creation Patterns

single    = 'Hello'
double    = "Hello"
multiline = """Line one
Line two
Line three"""

# Indexing and Slicing
word = "Python"
print(word[0])       # "P"  -- first character
print(word[-1])      # "n"  -- last character
print(word[2:5])     # "tho" -- slice
print(word[::-1])    # "nohtyP" -- reversed

# Operators
print("Hello" + " " + "World")  # "Hello World"
print("ha" * 3)                 # "hahaha"
print("py" in "python")         # True
```

Implementation and Code Examples

Example 1 -- Case, Testing, and Operators

This example applies case transformation and Boolean testing methods to a user-entered string. Every method call returns a new string without modifying the original.

```python
```

```python
# Example 1: Case Methods and Testing Methods

phrase = "  Hello, World!  "

# Case transformations
print(phrase.upper())       # "  HELLO, WORLD!  "
print(phrase.lower())       # "  hello, world!  "
print(phrase.strip())       # "Hello, World!"
print(phrase.strip().title())  # "Hello, World!"

# Testing methods
clean = phrase.strip()
print(f"isalpha: {clean.isalpha()}")   # False -- has comma, space, !
print(f"startswith H: {clean.startswith('H')}")
print(f"endswith !: {clean.endswith('!')}")
print(f"World in phrase: {'World' in clean}")
```

Expected Output

```
  HELLO, WORLD!
  hello, world!
Hello, World!
Hello, World!
isalpha: False
startswith H: True
endswith !: True
World in phrase: True
```

Example 2 -- Search and Replace

This example uses `find()`, `count()`, and `replace()` to analyse and clean a raw data string. Note that `find()` returns -1 when the substring is absent, which can be used in a conditional check.

```python
# Example 2: Search and Replace

text = "error: file not found. error: permission denied. error: disk full."
```

```
# Count occurrences
error_count = text.count("error")
print(f"Errors found: {error_count}")

# Find position of first and last occurrence
first = text.find("error")
last  = text.rfind("error")
print(f"First error at index {first}, last at {last}")

# Replace all errors with warnings
cleaned = text.replace("error", "warning")
print(cleaned)

# Find() returns -1 when absent -- safe to check
if text.find("critical") == -1:
    print("No critical errors.")
```

Expected Output

```
Errors found: 3
First error at index 0, last at 43
warning: file not found. warning: permission denied. warning: disk full.
No critical errors.
```

Example 3 -- Split, Join, and Text Parsing

This example demonstrates the split-process-join pipeline: break a string into a list, transform the list items, then reassemble into a new string. This pattern is a pattern you will encounter in almost every text processing task in Python.

```python
# Example 3: Split, Process, Join Pipeline

csv_line = "Fatima,28,engineer,london"

# Split into a list by the comma delimiter
fields = csv_line.split(",")
print(f"Fields: {fields}")
```

```
# Process each field -- capitalise with title()
formatted = [f.title() for f in fields]
print(f"Formatted: {formatted}")

# Reassemble with a different separator
result = " | ".join(formatted)
print(f"Result: {result}")

# Split on whitespace -- cleans multiple spaces automatically
messy = "  too    many   spaces  "
clean = " ".join(messy.split())
print(f"Clean: '{clean}'")
```

Expected Output

```
Fields: ['Fatima', '28', 'engineer', 'london']
Formatted: ['Fatima', '28', 'Engineer', 'London']
Result: Fatima | 28 | Engineer | London
Clean: 'too many spaces'
```

Example 4 -- Advanced f-String Formatting

This example demonstrates the full power of f-string format specifiers: width, alignment, padding, float precision, and thousands separators. These tools produce professional, column-aligned output without manual string padding.

```python
# Example 4: Advanced f-String Format Specifiers

items  = ["Widget", "Gadget", "Sprocket", "Thingamajig"]
prices = [9.99, 149.5, 0.75, 1200.0]
stock  = [100, 25, 8500, 3]

# Header with column alignment
print(f"{"Item":<14} {"Price":>8} {"Stock":>8} {"Value":>12}")
print("-" * 46)

for i in range(len(items)):
    value = prices[i] * stock[i]
```

```
    print(f"{items[i]:<14} {prices[i]:>8.2f} {stock[i]:>8,} {value:>12,.2f}")
```

Expected Output

```
Item           Price    Stock       Value
----------------------------------------------
Widget          9.99      100      999.00
Gadget        149.50       25    3,737.50
Sprocket        0.75    8,500    6,375.00
Thingamajig 1,200.00        3    3,600.00
```

Example 5 -- Complete Program: Text Analyser

This example builds a text analysis function that chains seven string methods to produce a structured report from a paragraph of raw text.

```
Python
# --------------------------------------------------
# Module  : text_analyser.py
# Purpose : Analyses a text string and reports stats.
# Author  : Ayman Alzaid
# --------------------------------------------------

def analyse_text(text):
    """Return a structured analysis of the given text string."""
    cleaned     = text.strip()                   # remove leading/trailing whitespace
    words       = cleaned.split()                 # split on whitespace
    sentences   = cleaned.count('''.'''".") + cleaned.count("!") + cleaned.count("?")
    unique_words = len(set(w.lower() for w in words))
    longest     = max(words, key=len)

    print(f"Characters : {len(cleaned):>6,}")
    print(f"Words      : {len(words):>6,}")
    print(f"Sentences  : {sentences:>6,}")
    print(f"Unique words: {unique_words:>5,}")
    print(f"Longest word: {longest}")
    print(f"Uppercase  : {cleaned.upper()[:40]}...")
```

```
sample = "Python is powerful. Python is readable. Is Python fun?"
analyse_text(sample)
```

Expected Output

```
Characters :      54
Words      :       9
Sentences  :       3
Unique words:      6
Longest word: powerful.
Uppercase  : PYTHON IS POWERFUL. PYTHON IS READABLE. IS...
```

The Active Learning Framework

Pillar 1 traces a string processing pipeline through method chaining. Pillar 2 presents four puzzles: immutability behaviour, split on different delimiters, find() vs index() on a missing substring, and f-string alignment edge cases. Pillar 3 audits a broken input validator with five violations.

Active Learning Pillars: **P1** Trace the interpreter line by line. **P2** Predict the output before running. **P3** Audit and refactor to PEP 8 standards. Verify every prediction at the terminal.

Pillar 1 -- Logic Exercise: String Pipeline Trace

String methods can be **chained**: calling one method on the result of another. Chaining reads left to right. Each method returns a new string, which the next method immediately receives. The original string is unchanged throughout.

PILLAR 1 Logic Exercise

Instructions: Trace the script below one statement at a time. For each assignment, record the exact string value stored. For each method call in the chain, record the intermediate result. Do not run the code.

Python

```
# Pillar 1: String Pipeline Trace

raw = "  HELLO, world! This is Python.  "

step_1 = raw.strip()
step_2 = step_1.lower()
step_3 = step_2.replace("python", "Python")
words  = step_3.split()
result = " -- ".join(words)

print(raw)     # original unchanged?
print(result)
```

String Pipeline Trace Table

Variable	Method Applied	Value After Operation
raw	(initial assignment)	" HELLO, world! This is Python. "
step_1	raw.strip()	? fill in
step_2	step_1.lower()	? fill in
step_3	step_2.replace("python","Python")	? fill in
words	step_3.split()	? fill in -- what type is this?
result	" -- ".join(words)	? fill in
print(raw)	--	? same as original or changed?
print(result)	--	? fill in final output

Challenge Questions: What type does split() return? Why is raw unchanged after all the processing? How many words does words contain and what separator does join() place between them?

Pillar 2 -- Mysterious Output Puzzles: Predict Before You Run

Four puzzles test the most common string mistakes. Predict all output before running.

PILLAR 2 Mysterious Output Puzzles
Instructions: Predict every line of output for each puzzle before running any code.

Puzzle 11.1 -- The Immutability TypeError

One of these four statements raises a TypeError. Identify which one and predict the output of the others.

```
Python
# Puzzle 11.1: Immutability

name = "Fatima"

new_name = name.replace("a", "A")  # A
print(name)                          # B
print(new_name)                      # C
name[0] = "A"                      # D -- predict the error
```

Questions: What do lines B and C print? Which line raises a TypeError and what is the error message? Why does .replace() work but index assignment does not?

Puzzle 11.2 -- split() Delimiter Behaviour

Predict all five outputs. Pay close attention to what happens when the delimiter appears at the start or end.

```
Python
# Puzzle 11.2: split() Edge Cases

print("a,b,c".split(","))
print("a,,b,,c".split(","))  # double delimiters
print(",a,b,c,".split(","))  # leading and trailing comma
print("hello world".split())
print("hello   world".split())   # multiple spaces
```

Questions: What does split(",") produce for double delimiters? Does the third call produce empty strings at the start and end? Do the last two calls produce the same result even with different amounts of whitespace?

Puzzle 11.3 -- find() vs index() on a Miss

Predict what happens for each of the four calls. Identify which one crashes and why.

```python
# Puzzle 11.3: find() vs index() on Missing Substring

text = "Python programming"

print(text.find("prog"))    # A
print(text.find("Java"))    # B
print(text.index("prog"))   # C
print(text.index("Java"))   # D -- predict the error
```

Questions: What does each call return or raise? Calls A and C search for the same substring -- do they produce the same result? What is the exact exception type raised by call D?

Puzzle 11.4 -- The f-String Alignment Surprise

Predict the exact output of each print. Use a ruler-style mental model: each field is exactly the specified width.

```python
# Puzzle 11.4: f-String Width and Alignment

n = 42
s = "hi"

print(f"|{n:8}|")       # int default alignment
print(f"|{s:8}|")       # str default alignment
print(f"|{n:08}|")      # zero-padded int
print(f"|{s:^8}|")      # centred string
print(f"|{3.14159:.3f}|")  # float precision
```

Questions: Integers default to right-alignment and strings to left-alignment -- do the first two lines confirm this? What fills the empty spaces in the zero-padded integer? How many decimal places does `:.3f` produce?

Pillar 3 -- Code Audit: String Handling Violations

The function below attempts to validate and normalise a username entered by the user. It contains five violations: attempting to mutate a string in place, using `index()` unsafely, building a result string with + concatenation in a loop (inefficient), no docstring, and ignoring the return value of strip(). Identify each violation, record it, and rewrite to production standards.

PILLAR 3 Code Audit -- String Handling

Instructions: Identify every violation. Record each in the audit table. Rewrite the complete function to production standards.

Non-Compliant Function

```python
def clean_username(raw):
    raw.strip()                     # BUG: return value discarded
    raw[0] = raw[0].upper()       # BUG: TypeError -- strings immutable
    pos = raw.index("@")            # BUG: crashes if @ absent
    result = ""
    for c in raw:               # BUG: use join() not + in loop
        result += c
    return result
```

#	Violation Found	Rule Broken	Corrected Pattern
1	raw.strip() return value discarded	Strings are immutable -- strip() returns a new string; the original is unchanged. Assign the result.	raw = raw.strip()
2	raw[0] = raw[0].upper() -- TypeError	Strings are immutable; character assignment is not allowed.	raw = raw[0].upper() + raw[1:] or raw.capitalize()
3	raw.index("@") crashes if @ is absent	index() raises ValueError if not found. Use find() and check for -1.	if raw.find("@") == -1: return None (handle the miss)
4	Building string with += in a loop	Performance: concatenation creates a new string each iteration. Collect in a list and join at the end.	Use "".join(list_of_chars) or simply return raw directly
5	No docstring	PEP 257: all functions need a docstring.	Add """Validate and normalise a username string."""

Production-Quality Refactored Function

```python
def clean_username(raw):
    """Clean and normalise a raw username string.

    Returns capitalised, stripped username, or None if invalid.
    """
    # strip() returns a new string -- must be assigned
    username = raw.strip()

    # Validate: must not be empty and must contain @
    if not username or username.find("@") == -1:
        return None  # signal invalid input without crashing

    # Capitalise by creating a new string (immutability respected)
    return username[0].upper() + username[1:].lower()

print(clean_username("  Fatima@example.com  "))
print(clean_username("no-at-sign"))
```

Coding Challenge: Password Strength Analyser

Chapter 11 Coding Challenge

Objective: Build a password strength analyser that uses string methods, testing methods, and f-string formatting to evaluate and score a user-supplied password.

>> Open with a PEP 8 compliant header comment block.

>> Collect a password string from the user using input().

>> Using string methods and Boolean testing, check five strength criteria: length >= 8, contains an uppercase letter (any(c.isupper() for c in pwd)), contains a digit (any(c.isdigit() for c in pwd)), contains a special character (any(not c.isalnum() for c in pwd)), and does not start or end with a space (use strip() comparison).

>> Count how many criteria pass and assign a strength label: 5 = "Very Strong", 4 = "Strong", 3 = "Moderate", 2 or fewer = "Weak".

>> Print a formatted report using f-strings with alignment: each criterion name left-aligned in a 25-char field, and PASS or FAIL right-aligned.

>> Include the final score and strength label in the summary.

Chapter Summary

Concept	Key Takeaway
Strings as sequences	Strings follow the same index and slice rules as lists. Index starts at 0. Negative indices count from the end.
Immutability	String characters cannot be changed in place. Every modifying method returns a new string. The original is always unchanged.
Operators	+ concatenates. * repeats. in tests membership. All return new values without modifying the original.
Escape sequences	\n is newline, \t is tab, \\ is literal backslash. Used inside string literals.
Case methods	upper(), lower(), title(), capitalize() -- all return new strings.
Testing methods	isalpha(), isdigit(), isalnum(), startswith(), endswith() -- return True or False.
find() vs index()	find() returns -1 on miss (safe). index() raises ValueError on miss (use when absence is an error).
replace()	Replaces all occurrences by default. Returns a new string. Does not modify original.
strip()	Removes leading and trailing whitespace. Must assign the return value -- the original string is unchanged.
split() and join()	split() breaks a string into a list. join() merges a list into a string. They are inverses.
f-string specifiers	:<10 left-align, :>10 right-align, :^10 centre, :0>5 zero-pad, :.2f float precision, :, thousands separator.
Method chaining	Methods can be chained: str.strip().lower().replace(). Each returns a new string for the next method.

CHAPTER 12

Dictionaries and Tuples

Learning Objectives

1. Explain what a dictionary is and why key-value mapping is more appropriate than indexing in many real-world scenarios.
2. Create dictionaries using literal syntax and the dict() constructor.
3. Access, add, update, and delete dictionary entries safely using bracket notation and dictionary methods.
4. Iterate over dictionary keys, values, and key-value pairs using keys(), values(), and items().
5. Use the get() method to access values safely without raising a KeyError.
6. Write dictionary comprehensions to build dictionaries from sequences in one expression.
7. Create and unpack tuples, and explain why tuple immutability makes them suitable as dictionary keys.
8. Apply tuple unpacking to receive multiple return values from a function cleanly.
9. Choose the correct data structure -- list, dictionary, or tuple -- for a given design problem.

Theoretical Foundation

The Limits of Indexed Access

Lists and strings access their elements by position. Position works well for ordered sequences where you need element 0, element 1, element 2. It breaks down the moment a program needs to look something up by a meaningful identifier. Storing a student's grade in a list requires remembering that index 3 means grade. Storing it in a dictionary means writing `student["grade"]` -- a line that reads like a sentence and requires no mental mapping.

A **dictionary** is a collection of **key-value pairs**. Each key is a unique identifier. Each value is the data associated with that identifier. Looking up a value takes the same time whether the dictionary has 5 entries or 5 million. This is the fundamental advantage over searching a list: the dictionary does not scan -- it jumps directly to the answer.

Figure 12.1 -- Dictionary Structure: Keys Map to Values

A dictionary holds pairs. The key on the left maps to the value on the right. Keys must be unique and immutable. Values can be any type.

student = { ... } -- a dictionary of 4 key-value pairs

Key	>>	Value
`"name"`	>>	`"Fatima"`
`"age"`	>>	`28`
`"grade"`	>>	`"A"`
`"active"`	>>	`True`

Keys must be immutable (str, int, tuple). Values can be any type. Insertion order preserved (Python 3.7+).

Dictionary Properties

Keys must be unique. A dictionary cannot have two entries with the same key. If you assign to an existing key, the value is updated -- no duplicate is created.

Keys must be immutable. Strings, integers, floats, and tuples can be keys. Lists cannot be keys because they can be changed after creation. A mutable key would break the internal lookup mechanism.

Values can be anything. A string, an integer, a list, another dictionary, a function. There are no restrictions on value types.

Insertion order is preserved. Since Python 3.7, dictionaries remember the order in which key-value pairs were inserted. Iterating over a dictionary visits keys in insertion order.

Safe Access: get() vs Bracket Notation

Accessing a key with bracket notation raises a `KeyError` if the key does not exist. The `get()` method is the safe alternative. It returns `None` by default if the key is absent, or a custom default value if one is provided as the second argument. In production code, `get()` is almost always preferred over bracket access for any key whose presence is not guaranteed.

Bracket Access vs get(): The Rule
Use dict[key]: when you are certain the key exists. A KeyError signals a programming error that should be visible.
Use dict.get(key): when the key might be absent. Returns None or your specified default. Never raises KeyError.
Use dict.get(key, default): `inventory.get("apple", 0)` returns 0 if "apple" is not in the dictionary.

Dictionary Methods

Method	Returns	Effect	Example
keys()	dict_keys view	All keys in insertion order	d.keys() >> dict_keys(["a","b"])
values()	dict_values view	All values in insertion order	d.values() >> dict_values([1,2])
items()	dict_items view	All (key, value) pairs as tuples	d.items() >> dict_items([("a",1)])
get(k, default)	Value or default	Returns value for k; default if absent (no KeyError)	d.get("x", 0)
update(other)	None	Merges another dict or iterable of pairs in place	d.update({"c": 3})
pop(k, default)	Removed value	Removes and returns value for k; default if absent	val = d.pop("a")
copy()	New dict	Shallow copy of the dictionary	backup = d.copy()
clear()	None	Removes all entries	d.clear()
setdefault(k,v)	Value	Returns value for k; inserts k:v if k absent	d.setdefault("count", 0)

Dictionary Comprehensions

A **dictionary comprehension** builds a new dictionary from an iterable in one expression. It mirrors list comprehension syntax but uses curly braces and requires a key-value pair separated by a colon.

```python
# Dictionary comprehension syntax
# {key_expr: value_expr  for  variable  in  iterable  if  condition}

# Example: square each number
squares = {n: n ** 2 for n in range(1, 6)}
print(squares)  # {1:1, 2:4, 3:9, 4:16, 5:25}

# With filter: only even numbers
even_sq = {n: n ** 2 for n in range(1, 11) if n % 2 == 0}
print(even_sq)  # {2:4, 4:16, 6:36, 8:64, 10:100}
```

Tuples: Immutable Ordered Sequences

A **tuple** is an ordered sequence like a list, but with one decisive difference: it is **immutable**. Once created, a tuple's contents cannot be changed. No appending, no removing, no item assignment. Attempting any mutation raises a `TypeError`.

The immutability of tuples makes them suitable for two specific roles that lists cannot fill. **First**: tuples can be dictionary keys, because they are immutable. Lists cannot. **Second**: tuples are the natural return type for functions that produce multiple values. When `divmod(17, 5)` returns `(3, 2)`, it returns a tuple. When `enumerate()` yields index-value pairs, each pair is a tuple.

Tuple Creation and Unpacking

Tuples are created with parentheses, or simply by separating values with commas. The parentheses are often optional, but they improve readability. A single-element tuple requires a trailing comma: `(42,)` is a tuple. `(42)` is just the integer 42 in parentheses.

Tuple unpacking assigns each element to a separate variable in one statement. The number of variables on the left must match the number of elements in the tuple. Unpacking works with any iterable, not just tuples, and is the standard way to receive multiple return values from a function.

Figure 12.2 -- List, Dictionary, and Tuple: When to Use Which

Three tools, three distinct roles. Use a list for ordered data accessed by position. Use a dictionary when you need to look things up by name. Use a tuple for a fixed record that must not change.

Property	List	Dictionary	Tuple
Syntax	[a, b, c]	{key: value}	(a, b, c)
Access by	Integer index	Key (any immutable type)	Integer index
Ordered	Yes (insertion order)	Yes (Python 3.7+)	Yes (insertion order)
Mutable	Yes	Yes (values and keys)	No -- immutable
Duplicate values	Yes	Values yes; keys must be unique	Yes
Use case	Ordered collection of items	Key-value lookup / mapping	Fixed record, function return, dict key

Formal Syntax and Declaration

Dictionary Creation and Access

Python

```python
# Dictionary Creation Syntax

# Literal syntax
student = {
    "name"   : "Fatima",
    "age"    : 21,
    "grades" : [88, 92, 79],
}

# Access by key -- raises KeyError if absent
print(student["name"])          # "Fatima"

# Safe access with get()
print(student.get("gpa", "N/A"))   # "N/A" -- key absent

# Add, update, delete
student["email"] = "fatima@nmsu.edu"  # add new key
student["age"] = 22             # update existing
del student["email"]          # delete a key

# Check existence before access
if "name" in student:
    print("name key exists")
```

Iterating Over Dictionaries

Python

```python
# Three iteration patterns

scores = {"Fatima": 88, "Hadi": 72, "Ellie": 95}

# Pattern 1: iterate over keys (default)
```

```
for name in scores:
    print(name)  # Fatima, Hadi, Ellie

# Pattern 2: iterate over values
for score in scores.values():
    print(score)  # 88, 72, 95

# Pattern 3: iterate over key-value pairs (most common)
for name, score in scores.items():
    print(f"{name}: {score}")
```

Tuple Syntax and Unpacking

```python
# Tuple creation
point      = (3, 7)            # two-element tuple
rgb        = (255, 128, 0)       # three-element tuple
single     = (42,)               # MUST have trailing comma
not_tuple  = (42)                # just an int in parentheses

# Tuple unpacking
x, y       = point                 # x=3, y=7
r, g, b     = rgb                   # r=255, g=128, b=0

# Unpacking function return values
quotient, remainder = divmod(17, 5)  # (3, 2)

# Tuple as dictionary key -- valid because tuples are immutable
location_data = {
    (40.7, -74.0): "New York",
    (51.5, -0.1): "London",
}
print(location_data[(40.7, -74.0)])  # "New York"
```

Implementation and Code Examples

Example 1 -- Building and Querying a Dictionary

This example builds a product catalogue dictionary, demonstrates safe and unsafe access patterns, and uses `update()` and `pop()` for batch modifications.

```python
# Example 1: Product Catalogue Dictionary

catalogue = {
    "apple" : {"price": 1.20, "stock": 100},
    "banana": {"price": 0.30, "stock": 250},
    "mango" : {"price": 2.50, "stock": 40},
}

# Safe access with get()
item = "mango"
info = catalogue.get(item, {})
print(f"{item}: ${info.get('price', 0):.2f}, stock={info.get('stock', 0)}")

# Add a new product
catalogue["grape"] = {"price": 3.00, "stock": 60}
print(f"Products: {list(catalogue.keys())}")

# Remove discontinued product
removed = catalogue.pop("banana", None)
print(f"Removed: {removed}")
```

Expected Output

```
mango: $2.50, stock=40
Products: ['apple', 'banana', 'mango', 'grape']
Removed: {'price': 0.3, 'stock': 250}
```

Example 2 -- Word Frequency Counter

A classic dictionary application: counting how many times each word appears in a text. `setdefault()` initialises a key to 0 if it does not yet exist, then the count increments. This pattern appears constantly in text analysis, log processing, and any task that counts occurrences.

```python
# Example 2: Word Frequency Counter

text = "to be or not to be that is the question"

frequency = {}
for word in text.split():
    frequency[word] = frequency.get(word, 0) + 1

# Print words that appear more than once
print("Words appearing more than once:")
for word, count in frequency.items():
    if count > 1:
        print(f"  {word!r:<10} x{count}")

print(f"Unique words: {len(frequency)}")
```

Expected Output

```
Words appearing more than once:
  'to'       x2
  'be'       x2
Unique words: 8
```

Example 3 -- Dictionary Comprehension

Dictionary comprehensions shine when transforming or filtering an existing data source. This example demonstrates three patterns: building from two lists using `zip()`, inverting a dictionary (swapping keys and values), and filtering to keep only high-scoring entries.

```python
# Example 3: Dictionary Comprehension Patterns
```

```
names  = ["Fatima", "Hadi", "Ellie", "Diana"]
scores = [88, 62, 95, 74]

# Pattern 1: build dict from two parallel lists
grade_book = {name: score for name, score in zip(names, scores)}
print(grade_book)

# Pattern 2: filter -- keep only scores >= 80
top_students = {k: v for k, v in grade_book.items() if v >= 80}
print(f"Top students: {top_students}")

# Pattern 3: invert -- swap keys and values
inverted = {v: k for k, v in grade_book.items()}
print(f"Score 88 belongs to: {inverted.get(88)}")
```

Expected Output

```
{'Fatima': 88, 'Hadi': 62, 'Ellie': 95, 'Diana': 74}
Top students: {'Fatima': 88, 'Ellie': 95}
Score 88 belongs to: Fatima
```

Example 4 -- Tuples: Unpacking and Dictionary Keys

This example demonstrates tuple creation, single-element tuple syntax, unpacking in three patterns, and the practical use of tuples as dictionary keys for coordinate lookup.

```
Python
# Example 4: Tuples -- Unpacking and as Dict Keys

# Basic unpacking
person = ("Fatima", 28, "Engineer")
name, age, role = person
print(f"{name} is a {age}-year-old {role}.")

# Swap two variables using tuple unpacking
a, b = 10, 20
a, b = b, a  # swap without a temp variable
print(f"a={a}, b={b}")
```

```
# Tuple as dictionary key (coordinate lookup)
grid = {
    (0, 0): "origin",
    (1, 0): "east",
    (0, 1): "north",
}
pos = (1, 0)
print(f"Position {pos} is: {grid.get(pos, 'unknown')}")
```

Expected Output

```
Fatima is a 28-year-old Engineer.
a=20, b=10
Position (1, 0) is: east
```

Example 5 -- Complete Program: Student Registry

This example builds a fully functional student registry using a dictionary of dictionaries. It demonstrates nested access, safe key checking, comprehension-based filtering, and formatted output -- all in a PEP 8 compliant module.

```
Python
# --------------------------------------------------
# Module  : student_registry.py
# Purpose : Manages student records using dictionaries.
# Author  : Ayman Alzaid
# --------------------------------------------------

registry = {
    "S001": {"name": "Fatima", "grade": 88, "active": True},
    "S002": {"name": "Hadi", "grade": 61, "active": True},
    "S003": {"name": "Ellie", "grade": 95, "active": False},
}

def print_registry(reg):
    """Print all active students with grades."""
    active = {sid: data for sid, data in reg.items() if data["active"]}
    print(f"Active students: {len(active)}/{len(reg)}")
    print("-" * 30)
```

```
    for sid, data in active.items():
        print(f"{sid}  {data['name']:<10}  Grade: {data['grade']}")

print_registry(registry)
```

Expected Output

```
Active students: 2/3
------------------------------
S001  Fatima      Grade: 88
S002  Hadi        Grade: 61
```

The Active Learning Framework

Pillar 1 traces a dictionary mutation sequence through a full state table. Pillar 2 presents four puzzles: the KeyError trap, dictionary key uniqueness, tuple single-element syntax, and iterating with items(). Pillar 3 audits a broken inventory counter with five violations.

Active Learning Pillars: **P1** Trace the interpreter line by line. **P2** Predict the output before running. **P3** Audit and refactor to PEP 8 standards. Verify every prediction at the terminal.

Pillar 1 -- Logic Exercise: Dictionary State Trace

Tracing dictionary operations requires recording the complete state of the dictionary after every mutation. Pay close attention to `get()` with a default (never raises an error), `pop()` (removes the key and returns its value), and duplicate key assignment (updates, does not duplicate).

PILLAR 1 Logic Exercise

Instructions: Trace the script below one statement at a time. Record the complete dictionary state after each operation. Record the value of any variable assigned from a dictionary operation. Do not run the code.

```
Python

# Pillar 1: Dictionary State Trace

inventory = {"apples": 10, "bananas": 5, "oranges": 8}
inventory["apples"] += 3
inventory["grapes"] = 15
x = inventory.get("mangoes", 0)
y = inventory.pop("bananas")
inventory.update({"oranges": 20, "limes": 6})
print(inventory, x, y)
```

Dictionary State Trace Table

Statement	inventory state after	Other variables
inventory = {...}	{"apples":10,"bananas":5,"oranges":8}	--
inventory["apples"] += 3	? fill in	--
inventory["grapes"] = 15	? fill in	--
x = inventory.get("mangoes",0)	unchanged	x = ? fill in
y = inventory.pop("bananas")	? fill in	y = ? fill in
inventory.update({...})	? fill in	--
print(inventory, x, y)	--	Output = ? fill in

Challenge Questions: What value does x hold and why? What does update() do when a key already exists (oranges)? What is the final state of inventory and the values of x and y?

Pillar 2 -- Mysterious Output Puzzles: Predict Before You Run

Four puzzles test the most common dictionary and tuple mistakes. Predict all output before running.

PILLAR 2 Mysterious Output Puzzles

Instructions: Predict the complete output for each puzzle. Record all predictions first. Then execute and compare.

Puzzle 12.1 -- The KeyError Trap

Predict which lines execute successfully and which raise a KeyError. For successful lines, give the exact output.

```python
# Puzzle 12.1: KeyError vs get()

config = {"debug": True, "timeout": 30}

print(config["debug"])              # A
print(config.get("debug"))           # B
print(config.get("port"))            # C
print(config.get("port", 8080))       # D
print(config["port"])               # E -- predict the error
```

Questions: What do lines A through D print? Which line raises a KeyError and what does the error message say? What is the difference between C and D?

Puzzle 12.2 -- Duplicate Key Assignment

Predict what the dictionary contains after all assignments and the final print output.

```python
# Puzzle 12.2: Duplicate keys -- what survives?

d = {"x": 1, "y": 2, "x": 3, "z": 4, "y": 5}
print(d)
print(len(d))
```

Questions: How many keys does the final dictionary have? What value does "x" hold -- 1 or 3? What value does "y" hold -- 2 or 5? What rule governs what happens when a key appears twice in a literal?

Puzzle 12.3 -- The Single-Element Tuple Trap

Predict the type and value printed for each of the four variables.

```python
# Puzzle 12.3: Single-element tuple vs parenthesised value
```

```
a = (42)     # parentheses only
b = (42,)    # trailing comma
c = 42,      # no parentheses
d = (1, 2, 3)  # normal tuple

for var in [a, b, c, d]:
    print(type(var).__name__, var)
```

Questions: Which variables are tuples and which are not? What makes b and c tuples when a is not? What is the minimum required to create a single-element tuple?

Puzzle 12.4 -- items() Unpacking in a Loop

Predict the exact output. Pay attention to how the tuple unpacking in the for loop interacts with the values inside each nested dictionary.

```python
# Puzzle 12.4: Iterating items() with nested values

prices = {"apple": 1.20, "banana": 0.30, "mango": 2.50}

total = 0
for item, price in prices.items():
    if price > 1.00:
        total += price
        print(f"{item:<10} ${price:.2f}  -- counted")
    else:
        print(f"{item:<10} ${price:.2f}  -- skipped")
print(f"Total (items > $1): ${total:.2f}")
```

Questions: Which items are counted and which are skipped? What does the final total print? What does each iteration of items() produce before being unpacked into item and price?

Pillar 3 -- Code Audit: Dictionary and Tuple Violations

The script below tries to count character frequencies from user input. It contains five violations: using bracket access without key checking (KeyError risk), using a list where a tuple should be used for a fixed coordinate record, no docstring, iterating with range(len()) instead of .items(), and a non-descriptive function name. Identify each, record in the audit table, and rewrite to production standards.

PILLAR 3 Code Audit -- Dictionary and Tuple

Instructions: Identify every violation. Record each in the table. Rewrite the complete script to production standards.

Non-Compliant Script

```python
def f(t):
    d = {}
    for c in t:
        d[c] = d[c] + 1      # BUG: KeyError on first occurrence
    keys = list(d.keys())
    for i in range(len(keys)):  # BUG: use .items()
        print(keys[i], d[keys[i]])

coord = [10, 20]  # BUG: should be a tuple
```

#	Violation Found	Rule Broken	Corrected Pattern
1	Function name f and parameters t, d, c are non-descriptive	Naming: use descriptive snake_case names	def count_chars(text): with freq, char, key
2	No docstring	PEP 257: all functions need a docstring	Add """Count character frequencies and print them."""
3	d[c] = d[c] + 1 -- KeyError on first occurrence	Safe access: use get() with a default of 0 to handle missing keys	freq[char] = freq.get(char, 0) + 1
4	range(len(keys)) with manual index lookup -- verbose and fragile	Style: use .items() to iterate key-value pairs directly	for char, count in freq.items(): print(char, count)
5	coord = [10, 20] -- mutable list for a fixed coordinate	Design: fixed records should be tuples. Lists can be mutated accidentally.	coord = (10, 20)

Production-Quality Refactored Script

```python
# --------------------------------------------------
# Module  : char_frequency.py
# Purpose : Counts and displays character frequencies.
# Author  : Ayman Alzaid
# --------------------------------------------------

def count_chars(text):
    """Count and print frequency of each character in text."""
    freq = {}
    for char in text:
        freq[char] = freq.get(char, 0) + 1  # safe: no KeyError

    for char, count in freq.items():  # clean iteration
        print(f"{char!r:<5}: {count}")

coord = (10, 20)  # tuple: immutable, correct choice for fixed record
count_chars("hello")
```

Coding Challenge: Contact Book

Chapter 12 Coding Challenge

Objective: Build a contact book application using a dictionary of tuples as its data model. Every requirement below must be satisfied.

>> Open with a PEP 8 compliant header comment block.

>> Store contacts as: contacts = {"name": (phone, email, city)}. The tuple value holds three immutable fields.

>> Write add_contact(contacts, name, phone, email, city) that adds or updates an entry.

>> Write find_contact(contacts, name) using get() that prints the unpacked tuple fields, or "Not found" if absent.

>> Write list_by_city(contacts, city) that uses a dictionary comprehension to build a filtered dict of contacts in the given city, then prints each one.

>> Write delete_contact(contacts, name) using pop() with a default, and print whether the deletion succeeded.

>> Use all four functions in a demonstration that adds at least four contacts, searches for one present and one absent, filters by city, and deletes one.

Chapter Summary

Concept	Key Takeaway
Dictionary	Key-value mapping. Keys must be unique and immutable. Values can be any type. Lookup is direct -- not sequential.
Creation	Curly brace literal {} or dict() constructor. Duplicate keys: last value wins.
Bracket access	dict[key] raises KeyError if key absent. Use when key is guaranteed to exist.
get()	dict.get(key, default) never raises KeyError. Returns default (or None) if key absent.
keys(), values(), items()	Three views for iteration. items() returns (key, value) tuples -- use for loops with unpacking.
update()	Merges another dict. Overwrites existing keys with new values.
pop()	Removes and returns the value. Accepts a default to avoid KeyError if key absent.
in operator	key in dict tests key existence without raising an error.
Dict comprehension	{k: v for k, v in ...} builds a new dictionary. Add if condition to filter.
Tuple	Immutable ordered sequence. Created with () and trailing comma for single element.
Tuple as dict key	Tuples are immutable so they can be dictionary keys. Lists cannot.
Tuple unpacking	a, b = (1, 2) assigns each element to a variable. Used for multiple return values.
Swap idiom	a, b = b, a swaps without a temp variable using tuple packing/unpacking.

CHAPTER 13

Exception Handling

Learning Objectives

1. Explain what an exception is, why exceptions exist, and how Python's exception mechanism differs from returning error codes.
2. Identify the eight most common built-in exceptions and describe the condition that triggers each one.
3. Write a correctly structured try/except block to catch and handle a specific exception type.
4. Use multiple except clauses to handle different exception types with different recovery strategies.
5. Apply the try/except/else pattern to separate error-handling code from normal-flow code.
6. Use the finally clause to guarantee cleanup code executes regardless of whether an exception occurred.
7. Use the raise statement to signal an error condition deliberately from inside a function.
8. Define a custom exception class by inheriting from Exception.
9. Distinguish between the LBYL and EAFP coding philosophies and explain when each is appropriate in Python.

Theoretical Foundation

What Is an Exception?

Every program written so far has assumed that inputs are valid, files exist, and arithmetic produces meaningful results. Real programs operate in an unpredictable world. A user types letters where a number is expected. A file has been deleted since the last run. A network connection drops mid-transfer. A list index goes out of range because the data was shorter than expected. These are not programming errors in the traditional sense. They are **exceptional conditions** -- events that cannot be handled by normal sequential logic.

Python responds to these conditions by **raising an exception**. An exception is an object that represents an error event. When Python raises an exception, normal execution stops immediately. Python searches backward through the call stack for a handler. If no handler is found, the program terminates and prints a **traceback** -- the sequence of function calls that led to the error.

Exception handling is the mechanism that intercepts an exception before it terminates the program. It allows the program to respond to the error, recover if possible, and continue running or exit gracefully with a meaningful message.

The Exception Hierarchy

Every exception in Python is an object that belongs to a class. These classes are organised in an inheritance hierarchy. At the top is `BaseException`. Below it is `Exception`, which is the base class for all common runtime errors. The eight exceptions you will encounter most frequently all inherit from `Exception`. Catching `Exception` catches all of them at once.

Figure 13.1 -- Python Exception Class Hierarchy

BaseException			
inherits from BaseException			
Exception	SystemExit	KeyboardInterrupt	
common runtime exceptions	*signals sys.exit()*	*Ctrl+C interrupt*	
ValueError	TypeError	ZeroDivisionError	IndexError
KeyError	FileNotFoundError	NameError	AttributeError

All common runtime exceptions inherit from Exception. Catching Exception catches all of them.

The Eight Most Common Exceptions

Exception	Raised When...	Common Trigger Example
ValueError	A function receives an argument of the right type but wrong value	int("hello") -- string that is not a number
TypeError	An operation is applied to an incompatible type	"5" + 5 -- cannot add string and int
ZeroDivisionError	Division or modulo by zero	10 / 0
IndexError	Sequence index is out of range	[1,2,3][10] -- index beyond list length
KeyError	Dictionary key does not exist	d["missing_key"] -- key absent from dict
FileNotFoundError	File or directory does not exist	open("no_such_file.txt")
NameError	Variable is referenced before assignment	print(undefined_var)
AttributeError	Attribute does not exist on an object	"hello".nonexistent_method()

The try/except Structure

The `try` block contains the code that might raise an exception. Python executes it normally. If an exception is raised, Python immediately stops executing the `try` block and jumps to the matching `except` clause. Code in the `except` block runs as the error handler. After the handler completes, execution resumes at the statement *after* the entire try/except structure.

Each `except` clause specifies which exception type it handles. Only the first matching `except` clause fires. A bare `except:` without a type catches everything -- this is almost always wrong. It hides unexpected bugs and makes debugging extremely difficult. Always name the specific exception type you expect.

else, finally, and raise

The else clause runs when the `try` block completes without raising any exception. It separates the "normal flow" code from the "exception handling" code clearly. Code that should only run when everything succeeded belongs in `else`, not at the bottom of the `try` block. This distinction matters because code in the bottom of `try` is *also* protected by the except clause, while code in `else` is not.

The finally clause runs *always* -- whether the `try` block succeeded, raised an exception, or even if a `return` statement was reached inside the `try` block. It is the guaranteed cleanup mechanism. Use it to close files, release database connections, or restore state that must be reset regardless of outcome.

The raise statement deliberately signals an error condition from inside your own code. Use it when a function receives input that is technically valid Python but violates the business rules your program enforces. Raising an exception is the correct way to communicate "this input is unacceptable" to the code that called your function.

Figure 13.2 -- try/except/else/finally Execution Flow

The diagram below shows which blocks execute under each outcome. The finally block always runs.

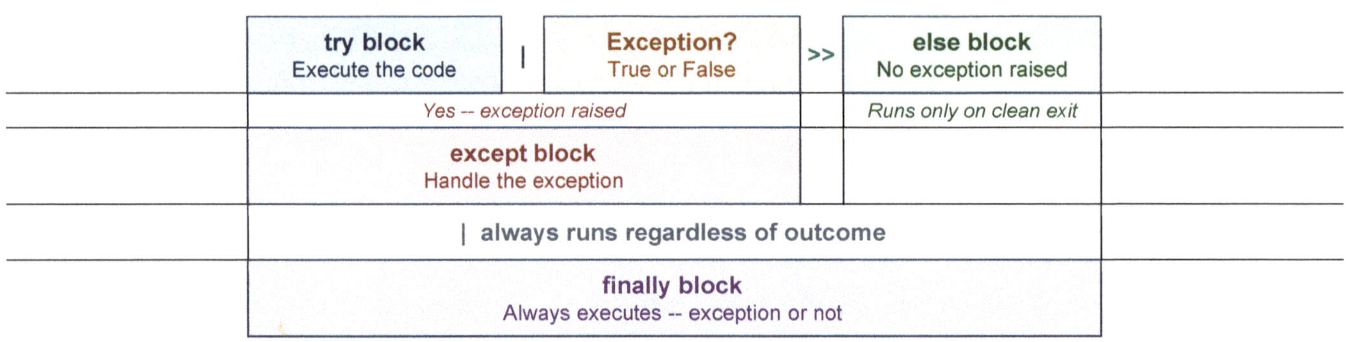

Custom Exceptions

A **custom exception** is a class you define that inherits from `Exception` (or a subclass of it). Custom exceptions make your code's error conditions self-documenting. When a function raises `InsufficientFundsError`, the caller immediately knows what went wrong and can write a specific handler for it. This is far clearer than raising a generic `ValueError` with a string message.

LBYL vs EAFP: Two Error-Handling Philosophies

LBYL (Look Before You Leap) checks conditions before performing an operation. Check if the key exists before accessing it. Check if the file exists before opening it. This is the dominant style in languages like C and Java.

EAFP (Easier to Ask Forgiveness than Permission) attempts the operation and handles any exception that results. Try to open the file; catch `FileNotFoundError` if it fails. Try to access the key; catch `KeyError` if it is absent. Python's standard library is designed around EAFP. It is generally preferred in Python code because it is faster (no redundant pre-check), and cleaner in concurrent environments where a pre-check result can become stale between the check and the action.

Style	Pattern	Example	When to Prefer
LBYL	Check first, then act	if key in d: val = d[key]	When the check is cheap and the failure case is common
EAFP	Act first, catch the exception	try: val = d[key] except KeyError: ...	When failure is uncommon and the check would duplicate logic

Formal Syntax and Declaration

try/except/else/finally

Python

```
# Full try/except/else/finally syntax

try:
    # Code that might raise an exception
    risky_operation

except ValueError:
    # Handles only ValueError
    print("Invalid value entered.")

except (TypeError, ZeroDivisionError) as err:
    # Handles multiple types; err holds the exception object
    print(f"Operation error: {err}")

else:
    # Runs ONLY if try block completed without any exception
    print("Success -- no exception was raised.")

finally:
    # ALWAYS runs -- exception or not
    print("Cleanup complete.")
```

raise and Custom Exceptions

```python
# Raise a built-in exception with a message
def set_age(age):
    """Set age after validating the range."""
    if not isinstance(age, int):
        raise TypeError(f"Age must be int, got {type(age).__name__}")
    if age < 0 or age > 150:
        raise ValueError(f"Age {age} is out of range (0-150).")
    return age

# Define a custom exception class
class InsufficientFundsError(Exception):
    """Raised when a withdrawal exceeds the account balance."""
    def __init__(self, amount, balance):
        self.amount  = amount
        self.balance = balance
        super().__init__(f"Cannot withdraw ${amount:.2f}; balance is ${balance:.2f}")
```

Implementation and Code Examples

Example 1 -- Basic try/except: Safe Input Conversion

The most common use of `try/except`: catching `ValueError` when casting user input. Without exception handling, any non-numeric entry crashes the program. With it, the program responds gracefully and can retry.

```python
# Example 1: Safe Integer Input with try/except

def get_int(prompt):
    """Keep asking until the user enters a valid integer."""
    while True:
        try:
```

```
            return int(input(prompt))
        except ValueError:
            print("Please enter a whole number.")

age = get_int("Enter your age: ")
print(f"In 10 years you will be {age + 10}.")
```

Expected Output

```
Enter your age: hello
Please enter a whole number.
Enter your age: twenty
Please enter a whole number.
Enter your age: 28
In 10 years you will be 38.
```

Example 2 -- Multiple except Clauses

Different exception types require different recovery strategies. This example handles a division operation that can fail in two distinct ways: a `ZeroDivisionError` when the divisor is zero, and a `TypeError` when a non-numeric argument is passed. Each except clause responds appropriately to its specific error condition.

```
Python
# Example 2: Multiple except Clauses

def safe_divide(a, b):
    """Divide a by b with full exception handling."""
    try:
        result = a / b
    except ZeroDivisionError:
        return "Error: cannot divide by zero."
    except TypeError as err:
        return f"Error: invalid types -- {err}"
    else:
        return f"{a} / {b} = {result:.4f}"

print(safe_divide(10, 4))
print(safe_divide(10, 0))
```

```
print(safe_divide("10", 4))
```

Expected Output

```
10 / 4 = 2.5000
Error: cannot divide by zero.
Error: invalid types -- unsupported operand type(s) for /: 'str' and 'int'
```

Example 3 -- else and finally in File Operations

File operations are the canonical use case for `else` and `finally`. The `try` block attempts to open and read the file. The `else` block processes the content -- it only runs if the file opened successfully. The `finally` block logs the attempt result, whether the file was found, missing, or any other outcome.

```python
# Example 3: File Read with else and finally

def read_config(filename):
    """Read and return config file content."""
    content = None
    try:
        f = open(filename, "r")
        content = f.read()
        f.close()
    except FileNotFoundError:
        print(f"Config file '{filename}' not found.")
    except PermissionError:
        print(f"No permission to read '{filename}'.")
    else:
        print(f"Loaded {len(content)} characters.")
    finally:
        print("Config read attempt complete.")
    return content

read_config("settings.txt")
```

Expected Output

```
Config file 'settings.txt' not found.
Config read attempt complete.
```

Example 4 -- raise and Custom Exceptions

This example defines a custom `InsufficientFundsError` and uses it in a bank account function. The caller catches this specific exception type and handles it with a user-friendly message. Specific custom exceptions produce cleaner, more informative error handling than generic ones.

```python
# Example 4: Custom Exception and raise

class InsufficientFundsError(Exception):
    """Raised when a withdrawal exceeds the balance."""
    def __init__(self, amount, balance):
        self.shortfall = round(amount - balance, 2)
        super().__init__(f"Need ${self.shortfall:.2f} more.")

def withdraw(balance, amount):
    """Withdraw amount from balance or raise custom error."""
    if amount <= 0:
        raise ValueError("Withdrawal amount must be positive.")
    if amount > balance:
        raise InsufficientFundsError(amount, balance)
    return round(balance - amount, 2)

try:
    new_balance = withdraw(100.00, 150.00)
except InsufficientFundsError as err:
    print(f"Declined: {err}")
except ValueError as err:
    print(f"Input error: {err}")
```

Expected Output

```
Declined: Need $50.00 more.
```

Example 5 -- Complete Program: Robust Data Processor

This example processes a mixed list of raw values, applying exception handling at every step. It demonstrates the EAFP philosophy: attempt the conversion, handle whatever fails, and continue processing. A `finally` block guarantees the summary is always printed even if an unexpected error occurs.

```python
# --------------------------------------------------
# Module  : data_processor.py
# Purpose : Processes raw values with full exception handling.
# Author  : Ayman Alzaid
# --------------------------------------------------

def process_values(raw_data):
    """Convert raw values to float, skip invalid entries."""
    results = []
    errors  = []

    try:
        for item in raw_data:
            try:
                results.append(float(item))
            except (ValueError, TypeError) as err:
                errors.append(f"{item!r}: {err}")
    except Exception as err:
        print(f"Unexpected error: {err}")
    finally:
        print(f"Processed: {len(results)} valid, {len(errors)} invalid")

    if results:
        print(f"Sum: {sum(results):.2f}  Avg: {sum(results)/len(results):.2f}")
    if errors:
        print(",","Skipped:", *errors, sep="\n  ")

data = ["3.14", "hello", 42, None, "7.5", "99x"]
process_values(data)
```

Expected Output

```
Processed: 3 valid, 3 invalid
Sum: 52.64  Avg: 17.55
Skipped:
  'hello': could not convert string to float: 'hello'
  None: float() argument must be a string or a number, not 'NoneType'
  '99x': could not convert string to float: '99x'
```

The Active Learning Framework

Pillar 1 traces exception handling flow through a script with multiple exception paths. Pillar 2 presents four puzzles: which except clause fires for a given exception, the finally guarantee, the else vs bottom-of-try distinction, and catching a parent class vs a child class. Pillar 3 audits a broken function with five exception handling violations.

Active Learning Pillars: **P1** Trace the interpreter line by line. **P2** Predict the output before running. **P3** Audit and refactor to PEP 8 standards. Verify every prediction at the terminal.

Pillar 1 -- Logic Exercise: Exception Flow Trace

Tracing exception handling requires following the flow through `try`, `except`, `else`, and `finally` for each specific input. Key rule: when an exception is raised inside `try`, execution jumps immediately to the first matching `except` clause. No remaining code in `try` runs. The `else` block is *skipped* when an exception occurs. `finally` runs in every case.

PILLAR 1 Logic Exercise

Instructions: Trace the function for each of the four test calls. For each call, record which blocks execute (try body, which except, else, finally) and the exact return value or output.

```python
# Pillar 1: Exception Flow Trace

def parse_score(raw):
    try:
```

```
        score = int(raw)
        result = 100 / score
    except ValueError:
        return "bad value"
    except ZeroDivisionError:
        return "zero score"
    else:
        return round(result, 2)
    finally:
        print(f"Attempted: {raw!r}")

print(parse_score("25"))   # Call A
print(parse_score("abc"))  # Call B
print(parse_score("0"))    # Call C
```

Exception Flow Trace Table

Call	Input	try body runs?	Which except fires?	else runs?	finally runs?	Return value
A	"25"	?	?	?	?	? compute 100/25
B	"abc"	partial	?	?	?	?
C	"0"	partial	?	?	?	?

Challenge Questions: For Call A: which line inside try raises no exception, so what does else return? For Call B: which line in try raises the exception -- int(raw) or 100/score? Does finally always print even when an exception is caught and the function returns a string?

Pillar 2 -- Mysterious Output Puzzles: Predict Before You Run

Four puzzles test the edges of exception handling. Predict all output before running.

PILLAR 2 Mysterious Output Puzzles

Instructions: Predict the complete output for each puzzle. Record all predictions first. Then execute and compare.

Puzzle 13.1 -- Which except Fires?

Only the first matching except clause fires. Predict what each of the three calls prints.

```python
# Puzzle 13.1: Which except clause matches?

def classify(x):
    try:
        result = int(x) / x
    except TypeError:
        print("TypeError caught")
    except ValueError:
        print("ValueError caught")
    except ZeroDivisionError:
        print("ZeroDivisionError caught")

classify(None)
classify("abc")
classify(0)
```

Questions: For classify(None): does int(None) raise TypeError or ValueError? For classify(0): int(0) succeeds -- which line inside try then raises ZeroDivisionError?

Puzzle 13.2 -- The finally Guarantee

Predict the exact sequence of lines printed. Pay close attention to when finally runs relative to the return.

```python
# Puzzle 13.2: finally always runs -- even before return

def test():
    try:
        print("try")
        return "from try"
    finally:
        print("finally")

result = test()
print(result)
```

Questions: In what order do the three print statements execute? Does finally run before or after the return value is sent to the caller? What does result hold and what is the final print output?

Puzzle 13.3 -- else vs Bottom-of-try

These two scripts look equivalent but behave differently when an exception is raised at a specific point. Predict both outputs.

```
Python

# Puzzle 13.3: else vs bottom-of-try -- spot the difference

values = ["5", "bad"]

# Script A: success_msg is inside try
for v in values:
    try:
        n = int(v)
        print(f"A: got {n}")
    except ValueError:
        print(f"A: error on {v!r}")

# Script B: success_msg is in else
for v in values:
    try:
        n = int(v)
    except ValueError:
        print(f"B: error on {v!r}")
    else:
        print(f"B: got {n}")
```

Questions: Do Scripts A and B produce the same output? Why might Script B's approach be safer if the print statement could itself raise an exception?

Puzzle 13.4 -- Catching a Parent vs Child Exception

Catching a parent class catches all its subclasses. Predict whether the more specific or more general except clause fires.

```
Python

# Puzzle 13.4: Parent class catches child exceptions
```

```python
def demo(x):
    try:
        result = int(x)
    except Exception:  # catches EVERYTHING
        print("Exception caught")
    except ValueError:  # never reached!
        print("ValueError caught")

demo("bad")
```

Questions: Which except clause fires? Is "ValueError caught" ever printed? Why not? What is the correct order -- should the specific exception come before or after the general one?

Pillar 3 -- Code Audit: Exception Handling Violations

The function below processes a list of prices but contains five violations: a bare `except:` clause that catches everything including keyboard interrupts, the exception object is caught but never used, the general `Exception` is placed before the specific `ValueError` (unreachable branch), no docstring, and catching exceptions that should never occur at that point (defensive over-catching). Identify each, record in the audit table, and rewrite to production standards.

PILLAR 3 Code Audit -- Exception Handling

Instructions: Identify every violation. Record each in the table. Rewrite the complete function to production standards.

Non-Compliant Function

Python

```python
def total_prices(items):
    total = 0
    for item in items:
        try:
            total += float(item)
        except Exception:             # BUG 1: too broad, before ValueError
            print("skip")
        except ValueError:             # BUG 2: unreachable
            print("bad value")
```

```
        except:                         # BUG 3: bare except
            pass
    return total
```

#	Violation Found	Rule Broken	Corrected Pattern
1	No docstring	PEP 257: all functions need a docstring	Add """Sum float values from items, skipping invalid entries."""
2	except Exception: placed before except ValueError:	Order rule: specific exceptions must come before general ones. Exception catches ValueError, making the second clause unreachable.	Swap order: except ValueError: first, then except Exception: if needed
3	except Exception: message just prints "skip" without showing what went wrong or which item	Best practice: always log the item and the error when skipping -- aids debugging	print(f"Skipping {item!r}: {err}") using as err
4	Bare except: catches everything including KeyboardInterrupt and SystemExit	Never use bare except. It swallows program interrupts and hides bugs. Always name the exception type.	Remove it. The except ValueError handles the intended case.
5	pass in the bare except silently discards all errors	Silent failure is dangerous. Every except should at minimum log what was caught.	Remove the bare except entirely. Log in the ValueError clause.

Production-Quality Refactored Function

Python

```python
def total_prices(items):
    """Sum numeric values from items, skipping non-numeric entries.

    Args: items (list): mixed-type list of values.
    Returns: float: sum of all successfully converted values.
    """
    total = 0.0
    for item in items:
        try:
            total += float(item)
        except (ValueError, TypeError) as err:
            print(f"Skipping {item!r}: {err}")  # informative, specific
    return total
```

Coding Challenge: Robust Student Score Importer

Chapter 13 Coding Challenge

Objective: Build a robust score importer that uses exception handling at every vulnerable point. Every requirement below must be satisfied.

>> Open with a PEP 8 compliant header comment block.

>> Define a custom exception InvalidScoreError(Exception) that stores the bad value and a message.

>> Write validate_score(score) that raises InvalidScoreError if score is not a number or is outside 0-100.

>> Write import_scores(raw_list) that calls validate_score() for each item in a try block, catching InvalidScoreError and ValueError separately with informative messages. Use else to append valid scores and finally to print how many items were processed.

>> Write a summary function that uses try/except to safely compute average, min, and max, handling the case of an empty list (ZeroDivisionError and ValueError respectively).

>> Demonstrate with a mixed list: [85, "ninety", 102, 67.5, None, "78", -5, 92].

Chapter Summary

Concept	Key Takeaway
Exception	An object that represents a runtime error. Raised when normal logic cannot handle a condition.
Traceback	The sequence of function calls printed when an unhandled exception terminates a program.
try block	Contains the code that might raise an exception. Execution stops at the first exception.
except clause	Catches a specific exception type and handles it. First matching clause fires. Always name the type.
as err	Binds the exception object to a variable: except ValueError as err. Use err to access the message.
else clause	Runs only when try completed without any exception. Separates success code from error handling code.
finally clause	Always runs -- exception or not, return or not. Use for cleanup: closing files, releasing resources.
raise	Deliberately signals an error: raise ValueError("message"). Use to enforce business rules.
Custom exception	class MyError(Exception): with a docstring. Makes error conditions self-documenting.
Exception ordering	Specific exceptions must come before general ones. Exception before ValueError makes ValueError unreachable.
Bare except	Never use except: without a type. It silently catches KeyboardInterrupt and hides all bugs.
LBYL vs EAFP	Check first (LBYL) or act and catch (EAFP). Python prefers EAFP: try the operation, handle what fails.

C H A P T E R 1 4

Object-Oriented Programming

Learning Objectives

1. Explain what object-oriented programming is and how it differs from procedural programming.
2. Define a class with the class keyword, including a constructor, instance attributes, and instance methods.
3. Explain the role of self in every method and why it is required.
4. Distinguish between instance attributes (unique per object) and class attributes (shared across all objects).
5. Implement the __str__ and __repr__ special methods to make objects printable.
6. Apply encapsulation using single and double underscore conventions.
7. Create a subclass that inherits from a parent class and extends it with new attributes and methods.
8. Use super() to call the parent class constructor and methods from a subclass.
9. Override a parent method in a subclass to produce different behaviour from the same method name (polymorphism).

Theoretical Foundation

The Limits of Procedural Programming

Every technique introduced in Chapters 1 through 13 belongs to **procedural programming**: writing instructions that execute in sequence, calling functions, handling exceptions, iterating over data. This model works well for programs with a clear, linear flow. It becomes difficult to manage as programs grow. A student record system has students, courses, grades, and instructors. Each concept has its own data (a student has a name, ID, and grade list) and its own behaviors (a student can enroll, withdraw, compute their GPA). Procedural code scatters that data across dictionaries and lists, and the behaviors across loosely connected functions. The relationship between the data and the code that operates on it is invisible.

Object-Oriented Programming (OOP) solves this by packaging data and behavior together. A **class** defines a blueprint: what data a thing holds (*attributes*) and what it can do (*methods*). An **object** is a concrete instance of that blueprint. Every student object has its own name, ID, and grades. The code that operates on those values lives inside the class itself. Data and behavior travel together.

Classes, Objects, and Instances

The distinction between a class and an object is the same as the distinction between a blueprint and a building. The blueprint defines the structure. Each building constructed from that blueprint is an independent physical object. Changing one building does not change the others or the blueprint.

In Python, a class is defined once with the `class` keyword. Objects (also called instances) are created from it by calling the class name as if it were a function. Each object has its own copy of all instance attributes. All objects share the same methods defined in the class.

Figure 14.1 -- Class as Blueprint, Objects as Instances

One class defines the structure. Many independent objects can be created from it, each holding its own data.

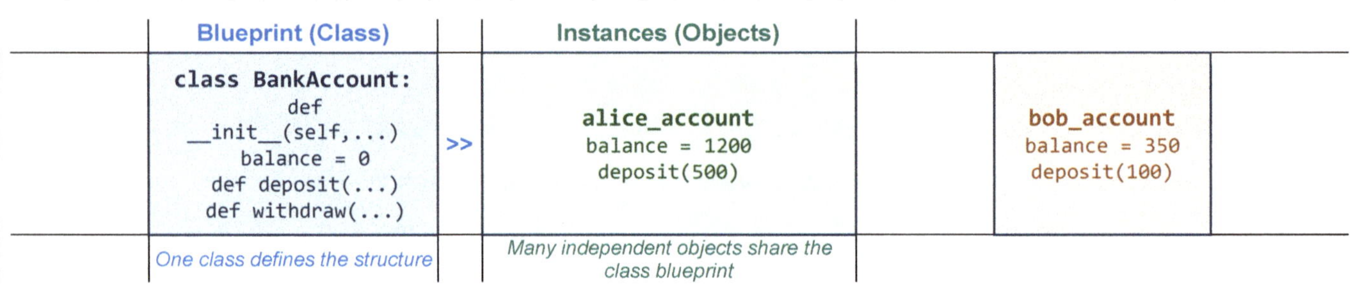

self: The Object Referring to Itself

Every method defined inside a class has `self` as its first parameter. When you call `account.deposit(500)`, Python translates this to `BankAccount.deposit(account, 500)`. The object itself is passed as the first argument automatically. `self` is the name Python convention uses for this parameter. It is not a keyword -- any name would work technically -- but `self` is universal convention.

`self` is how a method accesses the object's own attributes and other methods. Writing `self.balance` inside a method reads or writes the balance attribute of the specific object that called the method. Without `self`, there would be no way to distinguish one object's balance from another's.

The __init__ Constructor

The `__init__` method is the constructor. Python calls it automatically whenever a new object is created. Its purpose is to initialise the object's attributes to their starting values. Every attribute that the object will use should be defined here, not scattered across other methods. This makes the object's structure immediately visible.

Methods whose names start and end with double underscores are called **dunder methods** (short for double-underscore) or **magic methods**. Python calls them automatically in specific situations. `__init__` is called on object creation. `__str__` is called when you pass an object to `print()`. `__len__` is called when you use `len()` on an object.

Instance Attributes vs Class Attributes

Instance attributes are defined inside `__init__` using `self.attribute_name = value`. Each object has its own independent copy. Changing `Fatima.balance` does not change `Hadi.balance`.

Class attributes are defined directly in the class body, outside any method. They are shared across all instances. If you change a class attribute, the change is visible from every object unless that object has overridden it with its own instance attribute.

Instance Attribute vs Class Attribute
Instance attribute: defined with `self.name = value` inside `__init__`. Each object has its own copy.
Class attribute: defined at class body level with `name = value`. Shared by all instances. Useful for constants and counters.
Rule: When an instance attribute and a class attribute share the same name, the instance attribute takes precedence for that specific object.

Encapsulation

Encapsulation is the principle of controlling access to an object's internal data. Python uses naming conventions rather than strict access modifiers.

A single leading underscore (`_balance`) signals that an attribute or method is intended for internal use. Nothing stops outside code from accessing it, but the underscore is a contract: "this is not part of the public interface, use it at your own risk." Double leading underscores (`__balance`) trigger name mangling: Python renames the attribute to `_ClassName__balance`, making accidental access from outside the class unlikely. For most classes, a single underscore is sufficient. Use double underscores only when you specifically need to prevent a subclass from accidentally overriding an attribute.

Convention	Prefix	Meaning	Accessible From
Public	no prefix	Anyone can access and modify directly	Anywhere
Protected	_single underscore	Convention: internal use only. Not enforced by Python.	Technically anywhere, but "please don't"
Private	__double underscore	Name-mangled by Python to _ClassName__attr. Harder to access accidentally.	Only intended for use within the class

Inheritance and super()

Inheritance allows a class (the child or subclass) to acquire all the attributes and methods of another class (the parent or superclass). The child class can then add new attributes and methods, or override existing ones with new behaviour. Inheritance models the "is-a" relationship: a `Dog` is an `Animal`. It inherits everything Animal knows, then adds its own specific capabilities.

The `super()` function gives access to the parent class from inside the child. It is most commonly used in `__init__` to call the parent constructor: `super().__init__(...)`. This guarantees the parent's attributes are set before the child adds its own. Skipping the parent `__init__` is a common bug that leaves parent attributes uninitialised.

Figure 14.2 -- Inheritance: Parent Class to Subclasses

Child classes inherit all parent attributes and methods. They can override methods to produce different behaviour from the same name.

	Parent Class (Superclass)		Child Classes (Subclasses) -- inherit everything, add their own		
	Animal name, age speak() describe()	>>	**Dog** inherits all speak() >> "Woof!" fetch()		**Cat** inherits all speak() >> "Meow!" purr()
	shared attributes and methods		*speak() is overridden -- same name, different behaviour per class*		

Polymorphism

Polymorphism means "many forms". In OOP it means that different classes can implement the same method name and produce the right behavior for their specific type. A `Dog` and a `Cat` both have a `speak()` method. Calling `animal.speak()` on a list of mixed animal objects calls the right version for each one automatically. The calling code does not need to know or care what type each animal is. This makes adding new types straightforward: add a new animal class, implement `speak()`, and all existing code works with it immediately.

Formal Syntax and Declaration

Class Definition Syntax

```python
# Class Definition -- Formal Syntax

class ClassName:                    # PascalCase for class names
    """Docstring: what this class represents."""
```

```
    class_attribute = 0           # shared by all instances

    def __init__(self, param_one, param_two):
        """Initialise instance attributes."""
        self.attribute_one = param_one  # instance attribute
        self.attribute_two = param_two
        ClassName.class_attribute += 1  # update shared counter

    def instance_method(self):
        """A regular instance method."""
        return self.attribute_one

    def __str__(self):
        """Called by print() and str()."""
        return f"ClassName({self.attribute_one}, {self.attribute_two})"

# Create instances
obj_a = ClassName("value1", "value2")
print(obj_a)  # calls __str__ automatically
```

Inheritance Syntax

```
Python
# Inheritance -- Formal Syntax

class ParentClass:
    def __init__(self, name):
        self.name = name

    def describe(self):
        return f"I am {self.name}"

class ChildClass(ParentClass):  # inherits from ParentClass
    def __init__(self, name, extra):
        super().__init__(name)      # call parent constructor first
        self.extra = extra

    def describe(self):             # override parent method
```

```
        parent_desc = super().describe()  # call parent version
        return f"{parent_desc} with extra={self.extra}"
```

Implementation and Code Examples

Example 1 -- First Class: BankAccount

This example builds a complete `BankAccount` class from scratch. It introduces every core concept in order: `__init__`, instance attributes, methods, `__str__`, and a class attribute counter. Read the class definition fully before tracing the two object calls at the bottom.

```python
# Example 1: BankAccount Class

class BankAccount:
    """Represents a bank account with deposit and withdraw."""

    total_accounts = 0  # class attribute: counts all instances

    def __init__(self, owner, balance=0.0):
        """Initialise account with owner name and optional starting balance."""
        self.owner   = owner
        self.balance = float(balance)
        BankAccount.total_accounts += 1

    def deposit(self, amount):
        """Add amount to balance. Raises ValueError if amount <= 0."""
        if amount <= 0:
            raise ValueError("Deposit amount must be positive.")
        self.balance += amount

    def withdraw(self, amount):
        """Deduct amount if sufficient balance exists."""
        if amount > self.balance:
            raise ValueError(f"Insufficient funds. Balance: ${self.balance:.2f}")
        self.balance -= amount
```

```
    def __str__(self):
        return f"BankAccount({self.owner}, ${self.balance:.2f})"

Fatima = BankAccount("Fatima", 1000)
Hadi   = BankAccount("Hadi")             # default balance 0

Fatima.deposit(500)
Hadi.deposit(250)

print(Fatima)
print(Hadi)
print(f"Total accounts: {BankAccount.total_accounts}")
```

Expected Output

```
BankAccount(Fatima, $1500.00)
BankAccount(Hadi, $250.00)
Total accounts: 2
```

Example 2 -- Instance vs Class Attributes

This example makes the instance vs class attribute distinction concrete. Each student has their own `name` and `grade`. The class attribute `school` is shared by all instances and can be changed for all of them in one line.

Python

```
# Example 2: Instance vs Class Attributes

class Student:
    school = "Greenfield University"  # CLASS attribute

    def __init__(self, name, grade):
        self.name  = name    # INSTANCE attribute
        self.grade = grade

    def __str__(self):
        return f"{self.name} ({self.grade}) @ {self.school}"

s1 = Student("Fatima", "A")
```

```
s2 = Student("Hadi", "B")

print(s1)
print(s2)

# Change the class attribute -- affects ALL instances
Student.school = "Northside College"
print(s1)  # new school name appears
print(s2)  # same
```

Expected Output

```
Fatima (A) @ Greenfield University
Hadi (B) @ Greenfield University
Fatima (A) @ Northside College
Hadi (B) @ Northside College
```

Example 3 -- Inheritance and super()

This example builds an `Animal` parent class, then extends it with `Dog` and `Cat` subclasses. Each subclass calls `super().__init__()` to ensure the parent initialises its own attributes, then adds subclass-specific attributes. The `speak()` method is overridden in each subclass.

```python
# Example 3: Inheritance and Method Overriding

class Animal:
    """Base class for all animals."""
    def __init__(self, name, age):
        self.name = name
        self.age  = age

    def speak(self):
        return "..."  # placeholder -- subclasses override this

    def describe(self):
        return f"{self.name} (age {self.age}) says: {self.speak()}"

class Dog(Animal):
```

```
    """Dog inherits from Animal, adds breed, overrides speak()."""
    def __init__(self, name, age, breed):
        super().__init__(name, age)  # parent handles name and age
        self.breed = breed

    def speak(self):
        return "Woof!"

class Cat(Animal):
    """Cat inherits from Animal, overrides speak()."""
    def speak(self):
        return "Meow!"

animals = [Dog("Rex", 3, "Labrador"), Cat("Luna", 2)]
for animal in animals:
    print(animal.describe())
```

Expected Output

```
Rex (age 3) says: Woof!
Luna (age 2) says: Meow!
```

Example 4 -- Dunder Methods: __str__, __repr__, and __len__

This example shows how implementing dunder methods makes a class behave like a built-in type. `__str__` controls what `print()` shows. `__repr__` provides an unambiguous technical representation for debugging. `__len__` allows `len()` to work on the object.

```
Python
# Example 4: Dunder Methods

class Playlist:
    """A music playlist with dunder methods."""

    def __init__(self, name):
        self.name  = name
        self.songs = []

    def add(self, song):
```

```
        self.songs.append(song)

    def __len__(self):
        return len(self.songs)

    def __str__(self):
        return f"Playlist '{self.name}': {len(self)} songs"

    def __repr__(self):
        return f"Playlist(name={self.name!r}, songs={self.songs!r})"

p = Playlist("Chill Vibes")
p.add("Song A")
p.add("Song B")
p.add("Song C")

print(p)       # calls __str__
print(repr(p))  # calls __repr__
print(len(p))   # calls __len__
```

Expected Output

```
Playlist 'Chill Vibes': 3 songs
Playlist(name='Chill Vibes', songs=['Song A', 'Song B', 'Song C'])
3
```

Example 5 -- Complete Program: University System

This final example builds a small university class hierarchy. `Person` is the base class. `Student` and `Instructor` both inherit from it. This example applies every concept from the chapter in one coherent program: `__init__`, `super()`, instance attributes, class attributes, `__str__`, inheritance, method overriding, and polymorphism.

```python
# ------------------------------------------------------
# Module  : university.py
# Purpose : University person hierarchy using OOP.
# Author  : Ayman Alzaid
# ------------------------------------------------------
```

```
class Person:
    """Base class for all university members."""
    def __init__(self, name, email):
        self.name  = name
        self.email = email

    def greet(self):
        return f"Hello, I am {self.name}."

    def __str__(self):
        return f"Person({self.name}, {self.email})"

class Student(Person):
    """Student inherits from Person, adds ID and grades."""
    def __init__(self, name, email, student_id):
        super().__init__(name, email)
        self.student_id = student_id
        self.grades     = []

    def add_grade(self, score):
        self.grades.append(score)

    def gpa(self):
        return round(sum(self.grades) / len(self.grades), 1) if self.grades else 0.0

    def greet(self):  # override
        return f"Hi, I am {self.name}, student {self.student_id}."

class Instructor(Person):
    """Instructor inherits from Person, adds department."""
    def __init__(self, name, email, department):
        super().__init__(name, email)
        self.department = department

    def greet(self):  # override
        return f"Hello, I am Prof. {self.name}, {self.department} dept."

# Polymorphism: same greet() call, different behaviour
members = [
    Student("Fatima", "a@nmsu.edu", "S001"),
    Instructor("Dr. Smith", "s@nmsu.edu", "Computer Science"),
```

```
]

for m in members:
    print(m.greet())

# Student-specific behaviour
Fatima = members[0]
for s in [88, 92, 79, 95]:
    Fatima.add_grade(s)
print(f"Fatima GPA: {Fatima.gpa()}")
```

Expected Output

```
Hi, I am Fatima, student S001.
Hello, I am Prof. Dr. Smith, Computer Science dept.
Fatima GPA: 88.5
```

The Active Learning Framework

Pillar 1 traces a complete object lifecycle from instantiation through method calls and attribute changes. Pillar 2 presents four puzzles: the self mystery (what happens without it), class attribute mutation, calling the parent method via super() after overriding, and isinstance() with inheritance. Pillar 3 audits a poorly designed class with five violations.

Active Learning Pillars: **P1** Trace the interpreter line by line. **P2** Predict the output before running. **P3** Audit and refactor to PEP 8 standards. Verify every prediction at the terminal.

Pillar 1 -- Logic Exercise: Object Lifecycle Trace

Tracing an OOP program requires tracking the state of every object independently. Two objects of the same class hold separate copies of their instance attributes. When a method modifies `self.attribute`, only that specific object's attribute changes. Class attributes are shared -- a change to them affects all instances unless a specific instance has its own copy.

PILLAR 1 Logic Exercise

Instructions: Trace the script below one statement at a time. After each method call or attribute change, record the exact state of every object. Do not run the code.

```python
# Pillar 1: Object Lifecycle Trace

class Counter:
    total = 0  # class attribute

    def __init__(self, start=0):
        self.count = start
        Counter.total += 1

    def increment(self, by=1):
        self.count += by

    def reset(self):
        self.count = 0

a = Counter(10)
b = Counter()
a.increment(5)
b.increment()
a.reset()
b.increment(3)
print(a.count, b.count, Counter.total)
```

Object State Trace Table

Statement	a.count	b.count	Counter.total	Notes
a = Counter(10)	10	--	1	start=10 assigned; total incremented
b = Counter()	10	0	? fill in	default start=0; total incremented again
a.increment(5)	? fill in	0	2	only a.count changes

Statement	a.count	b.count	Counter.total	Notes
b.increment()	15	? fill in	2	only b.count changes; default by=1
a.reset()	? fill in	1	2	only a.count changes
b.increment(3)	0	? fill in	2	only b.count changes
print(a.count, b.count, Counter.total)	--	--	--	Output = ? fill in

Challenge Questions: Why does incrementing a not affect b.count and vice versa? After a.reset(), does b.count change? Counter.total counts how many Counter objects were ever created -- what is its final value?

Pillar 2 -- Mysterious Output Puzzles: Predict Before You Run

Four puzzles test the most common OOP mistakes. Predict all output before running.

PILLAR 2 Mysterious Output Puzzles

Instructions: Predict the complete output for each puzzle. Record all predictions first. Then execute and compare.

Puzzle 14.1 -- The Missing self

Predict what happens when self is omitted from a method. One of the two calls below raises a TypeError. Identify which one and explain exactly why.

```python
# Puzzle 14.1: What happens without self?

class Box:
    def __init__(self, width, height):
        self.width  = width
        self.height = height

    def area():  # BUG: missing self
        return self.width * self.height

b = Box(4, 5)
print(b.area())        # A -- instance call
```

```
print(Box.area(b))     # B -- class call with explicit object
```

Questions: Which call (A or B) raises a TypeError and which succeeds? When Python calls `b.area()`, how many arguments does it actually pass to the function? Why does Call A fail but Call B might succeed in this specific case?

Puzzle 14.2 -- Class Attribute Mutation via Instance

Predict all four print outputs. Pay attention to what happens to the class attribute when an instance assigns to the same name.

```python
# Puzzle 14.2: Class attribute vs instance attribute shadow

class Config:
    version = "1.0"  # class attribute

a = Config()
b = Config()

print(a.version, b.version)             # A

a.version = "2.0"  # create instance attribute on a only
print(a.version, b.version)             # B

Config.version = "3.0"  # change the class attribute
print(a.version, b.version)             # C
print(Config.version)                   # D
```

Questions: Lines B, C, and D are surprising to many students. Why does a.version not change at C even though the class attribute was updated? Why does b.version update at C even though b was not explicitly changed?

Puzzle 14.3 -- super() Calling the Parent After Override

Predict both print outputs. Trace exactly what super() returns and which describe() version runs.

```python
# Puzzle 14.3: super() after override
```

```
class Vehicle:
    def describe(self):
        return "I am a vehicle."

class Car(Vehicle):
    def describe(self):
        parent = super().describe()
        return f"{parent} Specifically a car."

class ElectricCar(Car):
    def describe(self):
        parent = super().describe()
        return f"{parent} Electric model."

c  = Car()
ec = ElectricCar()
print(c.describe())
print(ec.describe())
```

Questions: What do the two print statements output? When ec.describe() calls super().describe(), which class's describe() runs -- Vehicle's or Car's? How many times is the string "I am a vehicle." included in the ElectricCar output?

Puzzle 14.4 -- isinstance() and Inheritance

isinstance() is aware of the inheritance hierarchy. Predict all six outputs.

```
# Puzzle 14.4: isinstance() with inheritance

class Shape: pass
class Circle(Shape): pass
class Square(Shape): pass

c = Circle()

print(isinstance(c, Circle))   # A
print(isinstance(c, Shape))    # B -- is Circle a Shape?
print(isinstance(c, Square))   # C
print(isinstance(c, object))   # D -- everything is an object
```

```
print(issubclass(Circle, Shape))  # E
print(issubclass(Shape, Circle)) # F -- reversed
```

Questions: Why does B return True even though c was created from Circle, not Shape directly? Why does D return True? What is the difference between isinstance() and issubclass()?

Pillar 3 -- Code Audit: OOP Design Violations

The class below attempts to model a product in a store. It contains five violations: non-PascalCase class name, missing `__str__` method, a method that modifies `self` attributes without a docstring, a class attribute used where an instance attribute is needed, and direct attribute access from outside the class where a method should be called. Identify each, record in the audit table, and rewrite to production standards.

PILLAR 3 Code Audit -- OOP Design

Instructions: Identify every violation. Record each in the table. Rewrite the complete class to production standards.

Non-Compliant Class

```python
class product:                      # BUG 1: not PascalCase
    discount = 0                   # BUG 2: class attr, should be instance

    def __init__(self, n, p):     # BUG 3: non-descriptive params
        self.n = n
        self.p = p

    def apply_disc(self, d): # no docstring -- BUG 4
        self.p -= self.p * d

item = product("Laptop", 999)
item.p = 899                       # BUG 5: direct attribute manipulation
item.apply_disc(0.1)
print(item.n, item.p)
```

#	Violation Found	Rule Broken	Corrected Pattern
1	class product -- lowercase class name	PEP 8: class names use PascalCase	class Product:
2	discount = 0 as class attribute -- shared across all products	Design: each product should have its own discount. Use instance attribute in __init__.	self.discount = 0 inside __init__
3	Parameters n, p and attributes self.n, self.p -- non-descriptive	Naming: all identifiers must clearly describe their purpose	def __init__(self, name, price): with self.name, self.price
4	apply_disc has no docstring	PEP 257: all methods need a docstring	Add """Apply a fractional discount to the price."""
5	item.p = 899 -- direct external attribute modification instead of a method	Encapsulation: use a method to validate and set prices, never assign raw attributes from outside	Add a set_price(self, new_price) method with validation

Production-Quality Refactored Class

```python
class Product:
    """Represents a product with name, price, and discount."""

    def __init__(self, name, price):
        """Initialise product with name and price."""
        self.name     = name
        self.price    = float(price)
        self.discount = 0.0  # each instance has its own

    def set_price(self, new_price):
        """Set a new price after validation."""
        if new_price < 0:
            raise ValueError("Price cannot be negative.")
        self.price = float(new_price)

    def apply_discount(self, rate):
        """Apply a fractional discount rate (e.g. 0.10 for 10%)."""
        self.discount = rate
        self.price   *= (1 - rate)

    def __str__(self):
        return f"Product({self.name}, ${self.price:.2f})"

item = Product("Laptop", 999)
```

```
item.set_price(899)
item.apply_discount(0.1)
print(item)
```

Coding Challenge: Library Management System

Chapter 14 Coding Challenge -- Final Project

Objective: Build a complete library management system that demonstrates every OOP concept from this chapter. This challenge is the capstone exercise for the entire textbook.

>> Open with a PEP 8 compliant header comment block.

>> Define a base class LibraryItem with: title, author, year (instance attributes), is_checked_out = False, and a check_out() and return_item() method that toggle the flag and print a status message. Add a __str__ method.

>> Define a Book subclass that inherits LibraryItem and adds isbn and pages. Override __str__ to include the extra fields. Add a class attribute total_books that counts all Book instances created.

>> Define a Magazine subclass that inherits LibraryItem and adds issue_number. Override __str__ similarly.

>> Write a Library class that holds a list of LibraryItem objects. Add methods: add_item(item), find_by_title(title) using a loop with loop-else, list_available() using a list comprehension, and print_catalogue() using enumerate().

>> Demonstrate the system: create a Library, add at least 3 Books and 2 Magazines, check out two items, then print the full catalogue showing availability, search for a title, and call list_available().

>> Use isinstance() to distinguish Books from Magazines when printing the catalogue.

Chapter Summary

Concept	Key Takeaway
OOP	Packages data (attributes) and behavior (methods) together in a class. Models real-world entities naturally.
class	The blueprint. Defines what attributes and methods all objects of this type will have. Named in PascalCase.
object / instance	A concrete realisation of a class. Each object has its own copy of instance attributes.
__init__	The constructor. Called automatically on object creation. Initialise all instance attributes here.
self	The first parameter of every method. Refers to the specific object that called the method.
Instance attribute	self.name = value inside __init__. Each object has its own independent copy.
Class attribute	name = value at class body level. Shared across all instances. Changes affect all objects.
__str__	Called by print() and str(). Return a human-readable string representation of the object.
__repr__	Called by repr(). Return an unambiguous technical representation useful for debugging.
Encapsulation	_name convention: protected (do not use outside). __name: private (name-mangled by Python).
Inheritance	class Child(Parent): Child inherits all parent attributes and methods. Models "is-a" relationships.
super()	Calls the parent class method from inside the child. Use in __init__ to run the parent constructor.
Method override	Define a method in the child with the same name as the parent. Child version takes precedence.
Polymorphism	Different classes implement the same method name. One loop can call the right version for each type.
isinstance()	isinstance(obj, ClassName) returns True if obj is an instance of ClassName or any of its subclasses.

Appendix A Python Quick Reference

Built-in Data Types

Type	Literal Example	Notes
int	42, -7, 0	Whole numbers. No size limit in Python.
float	3.14, -0.5, 2.0e3	Decimal numbers. IEEE 754 double precision.
str	"hello", 'world'	Immutable sequence of characters. Supports indexing and slicing.
bool	True, False	Subclass of int. True == 1, False == 0.
list	[1, "a", True]	Ordered, mutable. Mixed types allowed.
tuple	(1, "a", True)	Ordered, immutable. Hashable if all elements are hashable.
dict	{"key": "val"}	Key-value mapping. Keys must be immutable. Insertion-ordered (3.7+).
set	{1, 2, 3}	Unordered, unique elements. Mutable. No indexing.
NoneType	None	Represents absence of a value. Used as a null sentinel.

Operators

Operator	Arithmetic	Operator	Comparison / Boolean
+ - *	Addition, subtraction, multiplication	== !=	Equal, not equal
**	Exponentiation (2**10 = 1024)	< > <= >=	Comparisons (return bool)
/	True division (always float)	and or not	Boolean AND, OR, NOT
//	Floor division (truncates to int)	in not in	Membership test
%	Modulo (remainder)	is is not	Identity test (same object)

Control Flow Syntax

Structure	Syntax Pattern
if / elif / else	if cond: / elif cond: / else:
while loop	while cond: ... (update variable inside body)
for over sequence	for item in iterable:

Structure	Syntax Pattern
for with counter	for i in range(n): or for i in range(start, stop, step):
break / continue	break exits the loop. continue skips current iteration.
loop else	else: block runs if loop ended without break.
match-case (3.10+)	match value: / case pattern: / case _: (wildcard)
try / except	try: / except ExcType as e: / else: / finally:
raise	raise ValueError("message")
def function	def name(params): / return value
class	class Name(Parent): / def __init__(self, ...):

Key String Methods

Method	Returns	Method	Returns
s.upper()	Uppercase copy	s.lower()	Lowercase copy
s.strip()	Removes leading/trailing whitespace	s.split(sep)	List of substrings
sep.join(lst)	Joined string	s.replace(a,b)	New string with a replaced by b
s.startswith(p)	True/False	s.endswith(p)	True/False
s.find(sub)	Index or -1	s.count(sub)	Number of occurrences
s.isalpha()	All letters?	s.isdigit()	All digits?
s.title()	Title Case copy	s.capitalize()	First letter upper

Key List Methods

Method	Effect / Returns	Method	Effect / Returns
lst.append(x)	Adds x to end (in place)	lst.pop(i)	Removes & returns element at i
lst.extend(iter)	Adds all items from iter	lst.remove(x)	Removes first occurrence of x
lst.insert(i,x)	Inserts x before index i	lst.sort()	Sorts in place (returns None)
sorted(lst)	Returns new sorted list	lst.reverse()	Reverses in place
lst.index(x)	Index of first x	lst.count(x)	Count of x in list
lst.copy()	Shallow copy	lst.clear()	Removes all elements

Key Dictionary Methods

Method	Effect / Returns	Method	Effect / Returns
d.get(k, default)	Value for k, or default	d.keys()	View of all keys
d.values()	View of all values	d.items()	View of (key,value) pairs
d.update(other)	Merge other into d	d.pop(k)	Remove & return value for k
d.copy()	Shallow copy	d.setdefault(k,v)	Returns d[k]; inserts k:v if absent

f-String Format Specifiers

<table>
<tr><th>Specifier</th><th>Meaning</th><th>Example</th><th>Output</th></tr>
<tr><td>:<10</td><td>Left-align in width 10</td><td>f"{'hi':<10}|"</td><td>hi |</td></tr>
<tr><td>:>10</td><td>Right-align in width 10</td><td>f"{'hi':>10}|"</td><td>   hi|</td></tr>
<tr><td>:^10</td><td>Centre in width 10</td><td>f"{'hi':^10}|"</td><td>   hi |</td></tr>
<tr><td>:.2f</td><td>Float with 2 decimal places</td><td>f"{3.14159:.2f}"</td><td>3.14</td></tr>
<tr><td>:,</td><td>Thousands separator</td><td>f"{1000000:,}"</td><td>1,000,000</td></tr>
<tr><td>:08</td><td>Zero-pad to width 8</td><td>f"{42:08}"</td><td>00000042</td></tr>
</table>

Essential Built-in Functions

Function	Returns / Effect	Function	Returns / Effect
len(x)	Length of sequence or dict	type(x)	Type object of x
range(n)	Integers 0..n-1	range(a,b,s)	Integers a..b-1 step s
int(x)	Convert to integer	float(x)	Convert to float
str(x)	Convert to string	bool(x)	Convert to Boolean
print(*args)	Prints to stdout	input(prompt)	Reads string from stdin
abs(x)	Absolute value	round(x,n)	Round to n decimal places
min(iter)	Smallest element	max(iter)	Largest element
sum(iter)	Sum of elements	sorted(iter)	New sorted list
enumerate(iter)	(index, value) pairs	zip(a,b)	Paired tuples from two iterables
isinstance(x,T)	True if x is instance of T	id(x)	Object identity (memory address)

Appendix B Common Runtime Error Guide

Twelve errors. Between them, they account for the majority of what you will see in your first year of writing Python. For each: what triggers it, a minimal example that reproduces it, and the fix. When your terminal shows an error, find it here first.

Exception	Triggered When	Minimal Example	Fix
`ValueError`	A function receives an argument of the correct type but an unacceptable value.	`int("hello")` `float("abc")`	Validate input before conversion. Wrap in try/except ValueError.
`TypeError`	An operation is applied to an incompatible type.	`"5" + 5` `len(42)`	Check types with isinstance(). Convert explicitly: int("5") + 5.
`ZeroDivisionError`	Division or modulo by zero.	`10 / 0` `100 % 0`	Guard with: if divisor != 0: before dividing.
`IndexError`	A sequence index is outside the valid range.	`lst = [1,2,3]` `lst[10]`	Check len(lst) before indexing. Use negative indices carefully.
`KeyError`	A dictionary key does not exist.	`d = {"a":1}` `d["b"]`	Use d.get("b") for safe access. Check "b" in d before bracket access.
`NameError`	A variable is referenced before it has been assigned.	`print(undefined_var)`	Ensure the variable is assigned before use. Check spelling.
`AttributeError`	An attribute or method does not exist on an object.	`"hello".nonexistent()` `42.upper()`	Verify the object type with type(). Check spelling of the attribute name.
`FileNotFoundError`	A file path does not exist or is misspelled.	`open("missing.txt")`	Check the path with os.path.exists(). Use try/except FileNotFoundError.
`IndentationError`	Code is incorrectly indented (mixed tabs/spaces or wrong level).	`def f():` `print("hi")`	Use 4 spaces consistently. Never mix tabs and spaces. Check all indentation levels.
`SyntaxError`	The code violates Python grammar rules.	`if x = 5:` `print "hi"`	Read the error message -- it gives the line number. Common causes: = instead of ==, missing colon, missing parenthesis.
`RecursionError`	A recursive function has no base case or the base case is never reached.	`def f(n): return f(n)` `f(1)`	Every recursive function must have a base case that stops the recursion.

Exception	Triggered When	Minimal Example	Fix
`OverflowError`	A float calculation produces a result too large to represent.	`import math` `math.exp(1000)`	Python integers never overflow (arbitrary precision). Floats do. Check your calculation scale.

Glossary

Terms are listed alphabetically. Numbers in parentheses indicate the chapter where the term is introduced in depth.

Term	Definition
Algorithm	A finite, ordered sequence of steps designed to accomplish a defined computational goal. Every program is an implementation of one or more algorithms. (Ch 1)
Argument	A value passed into a function at the point of the call. Distinct from a parameter, which is the variable name defined in the function signature. (Ch 7)
Attribute	A variable bound to an object that stores state specific to that object. Defined with self.name inside a class. (Ch 14)
Boolean	A data type with exactly two values: True and False. Subclass of int in Python, where True == 1 and False == 0. (Ch 4)
Break	A keyword that immediately exits the nearest enclosing loop, transferring control to the first statement after the loop block. (Ch 9)
Built-in Function	A function provided by Python itself, available without importing any module. Examples include len(), range(), print(), and isinstance(). (Ch 8)
Call Stack	The runtime record of active function invocations. When one function calls another, a new frame is added. When the function returns, the frame is removed. (Ch 7)
Class	A blueprint that defines the attributes and methods shared by all objects of a given type. Instantiated with ClassName(). (Ch 14)
Class Attribute	An attribute defined in the class body outside any method. Shared across all instances. Distinct from instance attributes, which are unique per object. (Ch 14)
Comment	A line or portion of a line beginning with # that the interpreter ignores entirely. Used to explain intent or disable code temporarily. (Ch 1)
Comprehension	A compact expression for building a new list, dictionary, or set from an iterable. Example: [x**2 for x in range(10) if x % 2 == 0]. (Ch 10)
Conditional	A control structure that executes a block of code only when a specified Boolean condition evaluates to True. Implemented with if, elif, and else. (Ch 5)
Constructor	The __init__ method of a class, called automatically when a new object is created. Responsible for initialising all instance attributes. (Ch 14)
Continue	A keyword that skips the remaining statements in the current iteration of a loop and immediately starts the next iteration. (Ch 9)
Data Type	A classification that determines which values a variable can hold and which operations can be applied to it. Core Python types: int, float, str, bool, list, dict, tuple. (Ch 2)
Decomposition	The practice of breaking a complex problem into smaller, independent, solvable sub-problems before writing any code. Central to the software engineering mindset. (Ch 1)
Default Argument	A parameter value used automatically when no argument is supplied by the caller. Defined with parameter=value in the function signature. (Ch 7)
Dictionary	A mutable, insertion-ordered collection of key-value pairs. Keys must be unique and immutable. Accessed by key, not by position. (Ch 12)
Docstring	A string literal placed as the first statement of a function, method, class, or module. Describes purpose, parameters, and return value. Accessed via __doc__. (Ch 7)

Term	Definition
Dunder Method	A method whose name begins and ends with double underscores. Called automatically by Python in specific situations. __init__, __str__, and __len__ are examples. (Ch 14)
EAFP	Easier to Ask Forgiveness than Permission. A Python coding philosophy that attempts an operation first and handles any exception that results, rather than pre-checking conditions. (Ch 13)
Encapsulation	The practice of controlling access to an object's internal data. Python uses naming conventions: _name for protected, __name for private. (Ch 14)
Exception	A runtime event that disrupts normal program flow. Represented as an object that inherits from BaseException. Handled with try/except. (Ch 13)
Expression	A combination of values, variables, and operators that Python evaluates to produce a single value. 2 + 3 and len("hi") > 0 are both expressions. (Ch 2)
f-string	A string literal prefixed with f that evaluates embedded expressions at runtime. Introduced in Python 3.6. f"Result: {2 + 2}" produces "Result: 4". (Ch 3)
Finally	A clause on a try block that executes unconditionally, whether an exception occurred or not. Used for guaranteed cleanup. (Ch 13)
Float	A double-precision floating-point number. Stores decimals and very large or very small values. Subject to rounding errors inherent in binary representation. (Ch 2)
For Loop	A loop that iterates over each item in a sequence, executing its body once per item. Ends automatically when the sequence is exhausted. (Ch 9)
Function	A named, reusable block of code that accepts inputs (parameters), performs a task, and optionally returns a value. Defined with def. (Ch 7)
Immutable	A property of objects whose value cannot be changed after creation. Strings, integers, floats, booleans, and tuples are immutable in Python. (Ch 11)
Indentation	The leading whitespace at the start of a line. In Python, indentation is syntactically significant and defines the boundaries of blocks. Standard is 4 spaces. (Ch 5)
Inheritance	A mechanism by which a class (subclass) acquires the attributes and methods of another class (superclass). Enables code reuse and the "is-a" relationship. (Ch 14)
Instance	A specific object created from a class blueprint. Each instance has its own copy of instance attributes. (Ch 14)
Integer	A whole number of arbitrary size in Python. No overflow for int; size is limited only by available memory. (Ch 2)
Interpreter	A program that reads and executes source code directly, line by line, without compiling to machine code first. Python uses CPython by default. (Ch 1)
KeyError	A runtime exception raised when a dictionary key that does not exist is accessed using bracket notation. Avoided by using .get(). (Ch 12)
Lambda	An anonymous, single-expression function defined inline. Used when a full def statement would be verbose. sorted(lst, key=lambda x: x[1]). (Ch 8)
List	An ordered, mutable sequence that can hold elements of any type. Supports indexing, slicing, and a rich set of mutation methods. (Ch 10)
List Comprehension	See Comprehension. (Ch 10)
Loop	A control structure that executes a block of code repeatedly. Python provides while (condition-based) and for (iteration-based) loops. (Ch 9)
Match-Case	A structural pattern matching statement introduced in Python 3.10. Compares a value against patterns and executes the first matching case block. (Ch 6)

Term	Definition
Method	A function defined inside a class body. Always receives self as its first parameter, which refers to the calling object. (Ch 14)
Module	A Python source file containing definitions and statements. Imported into other files with import. The standard library is a collection of modules. (Ch 1)
Mutable	A property of objects whose contents can be changed after creation. Lists, dictionaries, and sets are mutable. (Ch 10)
None	Python's null value. Represents the absence of a meaningful result. Functions without an explicit return statement return None. Type is NoneType. (Ch 7)
Object	An instance of a class. Every value in Python is an object, including integers and strings. Objects have a type, an identity, and a value. (Ch 14)
Parameter	A variable name in a function definition that receives an argument value when the function is called. (Ch 7)
PEP 8	Python Enhancement Proposal 8. The official style guide for Python code. Covers naming, indentation, line length, and documentation standards. (Ch 8)
Polymorphism	The ability of different classes to implement the same method name with different behaviour. Allows code to operate on objects without knowing their specific type. (Ch 14)
Raise	A statement that deliberately signals an exception. Used to enforce business rules or signal error conditions from inside a function. (Ch 13)
Range	A built-in type that generates an immutable sequence of integers on demand. Memory-efficient: range(1000000) stores only start, stop, and step. (Ch 9)
Recursion	A technique where a function calls itself as part of its own body. Requires a base case to prevent infinite execution. (Ch 7)
Return	A statement that exits the current function and sends a value back to the caller. A function without return implicitly returns None. (Ch 7)
Scope	The region of code where a variable name is visible. Python uses LEGB resolution: Local, Enclosing, Global, Built-in. (Ch 7)
Self	The conventional name for the first parameter of a method, which receives the object that called the method. Not a keyword, but universal convention. (Ch 14)
Slice	A sub-sequence extracted from a list or string using [start:stop:step] notation. The stop index is never included. (Ch 10, 11)
String	An immutable, ordered sequence of Unicode characters. Accessed via indexing and slicing. The primary text data type. (Ch 11)
super()	A function that returns a proxy to the parent class, used to call parent methods from within a subclass. Essential in __init__ overrides. (Ch 14)
Traceback	The formatted error output Python displays when an unhandled exception terminates a program. Shows the call stack and the exact error type and message. (Ch 13)
Tuple	An ordered, immutable sequence. Lighter than a list. Suitable as dictionary keys and function return values. Single-element tuple requires a trailing comma. (Ch 12)
Type Conversion	Explicitly changing a value from one type to another. int("5"), float(3), and str(42) are common examples. Implicit conversion does not occur in Python. (Ch 2)
Variable	A named reference to a value stored in memory. Created by assignment: name = value. Python uses dynamic typing -- the type is determined by the value, not the variable. (Ch 2)
While Loop	A loop that continues executing as long as its condition evaluates to True. Requires initialisation before the loop and an update inside the body. (Ch 9)

www.ingramcontent.com/pod-product-compliance
Lightning Source LLC
LaVergne TN
LVHW070852210926
848482LV00016B/919

* 9 7 9 8 9 5 1 0 8 7 0 0 3 *